DISCOVERING THE GLORIOUS

GOSPEL

PAUL DAVID WASHER

"As expected, Paul Washer is a faithful guide through the key gospel doctrines in *Discovering the Glorious Gospel*. Here you will find faithful exegetical and theological explanation as well as helpful, guided questions and Scripture readings. This will be a very helpful tool for individual or group study, enabling people to delve more deeply into the glorious truths of who God is and how He has graciously acted to save us."

— Ray Van Neste, Professor at **Union University**, Contributor to the *ESV Study Bible*

•

"Paul Washer's book *Discovering the Glorious Gospel* is like a gust of fresh air from heaven. First, it is a workbook that challenges us to get into the Bible and learn the soul-nourishing truths of the gospel for ourselves. Paul Washer uses the rich concepts of the Bible to bring out the contours of the person and work of Christ until the gospel stands out like the awe-inspiring Mt. Everest. Second, this book takes us back to the foundational reason why God saves the way He does through the gospel: in order to glorify Himself. The book starts with the divine dilemma, and after all is said and done it leaves us on our knees worshiping the exalted God of grace and justice. If you want to know why the gospel is the greatest truth of all time, buy this book and study it with an open Bible in your hands!"

— Conrad Mbewe, Pastor of **Kabwata Baptist Church**, Author of *Foundations for the Flock*

DISCOVERING THE GLORIOUS **GOSPEL**

Published by:

HeartCry Missionary Society
PO Box 7372
Roanoke, VA 24019

www.heartcrymissionary.com

Printed in the United States of America 2023
Fourth Edition, Second Printing

Unless otherwise noted, all Scripture quotations taken from the
New American Standard Bible®
Copyright 1960, 1962, 1963, 1968, 1971, 1972, 1973, 1975, 1977, 1995
by the Lockman Foundation. Used by permission.

Edited by Forrest Hite and Meghan Nash
Layout and design by Jon Green, Matthew Robinson, Forrest Hite, and Michael Reece

DISCOVERING THE GLORIOUS GOSPEL

Table of Contents

Introduction

METHOD OF STUDY

The great goal of this study is for the student to have an encounter with God through His Word. Founded upon the conviction that the Scriptures are the inspired and infallible Word of God, this study has been designed in such a way that it is literally impossible for the student to advance without an open Bible before him or her. The goal is to help the reader obey the exhortation of the Apostle Paul in II Timothy 2:15:

> *Be diligent to present yourself approved to God as a workman who does not need to be ashamed, accurately handling the word of truth.*

Each chapter deals with a specific aspect of the gospel of Jesus Christ. The student will complete each chapter by answering the questions and following the instructions according to the Scriptures given. The student is encouraged to meditate upon each text and write his or her thoughts. The benefit gained from this study will depend upon the student's investment. If the student answers the questions thoughtlessly, merely copying the text without seeking to understand its meaning, this book will be of very little help.

Discovering the Glorious Gospel is primarily a biblical study and does not contain much in the way of colorful illustrations, quaint stories, or even theological commentaries. It was the desire of the author to provide a work that simply points the way to the Scriptures and allows the Word of God to speak for itself.

This workbook may be used by an individual, in a small group, for a Sunday school class, or in other contexts. It is highly recommended that the student complete each chapter on his or her own before meeting for discussion and questions with the group or discipleship leader.

EXHORTATION TO THE STUDENT

The student is encouraged to study biblical doctrine and discover its exalted place in the Christian life. The true Christian cannot bear or even survive a divorce between the emotions and the intellect or between devotion to God and the doctrine of God. According to the Scriptures, neither our emotions nor our experiences provide an adequate foundation for the Christian life. Only the truths of Scripture, understood with the mind and communicated through doctrine, can provide that sure foundation upon which we should establish our beliefs and our behavior and determine the validity of our emotions and experiences. The mind is not the enemy of the heart, and doctrine is not an obstacle to devotion. The two are indispensable and should be inseparable. The Scriptures command us to love the Lord our God with all our heart, with all our soul, and with all our mind (Matthew 22:37) and to worship God both in spirit and in truth (John 4:24).

The study of doctrine is both an intellectual and devotional discipline. It is a passionate search for God that should always lead the student to greater personal transformation, obedience, and heartfelt worship. Therefore, the student should be on guard against the great error of seeking only impersonal knowledge instead of the person of God. Neither mindless devotion nor mere intellectual pursuits are profitable, for in either case, God is lost.

THE NEW AMERICAN STANDARD BIBLE

The New American Standard Bible (1995 edition) is required to complete this study. This version of Scripture was chosen for the following reasons: (1) the unwavering conviction of its translators that the Bible is the infallible Word of God; and (2) its faithfulness to the original languages. This workbook is also available for use with the English Standard Version and the King James Version (heartcrymissionary.com/books).

A WORD FROM THE AUTHOR

The death and resurrection of Jesus Christ is the center of human history, the greatest story ever told, and the subject of angelic contemplation (I Peter 1:12). When proclaimed with biblical fidelity, it is the power of God for salvation to everyone who believes (Romans 1:16) and the great source and motivation of all true piety (I Timothy 3:16). When its message is distorted, it brings death to the hearers and the gravest of curses to the one who proclaims it (Galatians 1:6-9). For these reasons and many others, the Christian should consider his or her study of the gospel to be a primary and lifelong task. This workbook was designed and written with these things in mind.

I would like to thank my wife Charo for her constant support and my four children (Ian, Evan, Rowan, and Bronwyn), who continue to be a great delight. I would also like to thank HeartCry staff member Forrest Hite for his diligent and meticulous editing of the several different manuscripts that he has received. His contributions to the arrangement and overall readability of this work are as significant as they are appreciated. My thanks also are extended to the entire staff at HeartCry, who have been a great encouragement throughout the process of this book's publication.

RECOMMENDED RESOURCES FOR FURTHER STUDIES

What Is the Gospel? by Greg Gilbert
Fifty Reasons Why Jesus Came to Die by John Piper
Saved by Grace by Anthony Hoekema
Redemption Accomplished and Applied by John Murray
The Cross of Christ by John R. W. Stott
The Gospel's Power and Message by Paul David Washer
The Gospel and True Conversion by Paul David Washer
Gospel Assurance and Warnings by Paul David Washer
The Death of Death in the Death of Christ by John Owen (for advanced students)

ADDITIONAL NOTE

You may have noticed that this book is being sold at a strange price. Here's why: one dollar ($) from every copy sold will go directly to fund mission work through HeartCry Missionary Society (heartcrymissionary.com). The rest of the sale price is just enough to cover the cost of printing, publication, and distribution. The author is not profiting from the sale of this book, nor has he profited from the sale of any other book. Over the years, we have utilized and explored many avenues in order to publish these workbooks. Ultimately, we have reached the conclusion that doing so in-house at a low cost, even with slightly lower quality, is the most effective way of getting these useful tools into the hands of as many people across the globe as possible. We hope and pray that the Lord continues to use these books to point His people to His Word unto the edification of His church.

Optional Study Schedule

Week One: The Divine Dilemma and God's Gospel Motivation
  Day 1:   Chapter 1
  Day 2:   Chapter 2, Section 1
  Day 3:   Chapter 2, Section 2
  Day 4:   Chapter 3, Sections 1-2
  Day 5:   Chapter 3, Section 3

Week Two: The Son's Incarnation and Life
  Day 1:   Chapter 4
  Day 2:   Chapter 5
  Day 3:   Chapter 6
  Day 4:   Chapter 7, Main Points 1-5
  Day 5:   Chapter 7, Main Points 6-7

Week Three: The Son's Suffering and Death
  Day 1:   Chapter 8
  Day 2:   Chapter 9
  Day 3:   Chapter 10, Section 1
  Day 4:   Chapter 10, Section 2
  Day 5:   Chapter 11

Week Four: The Importance of Christ's Life and Death
  Day 1:   Chapter 12
  Day 2:   Chapter 13
  Day 3:   Chapter 14
  Day 4:   Chapter 15
  Day 5:   Chapter 16

Week Five: The Importance of Christ as the Sacrifice
  Day 1:   Chapter 17, Main Points 1-2
  Day 2:   Chapter 17, Main Points 3-4
  Day 3:   Chapter 18, Section 1
  Day 4:   Chapter 18, Section 2
           Chapter 19, Section 1
  Day 5:   Chapter 19, Sections 2-3

Week Six: The Son's Burial and Resurrection
  Day 1:   Chapter 20
  Day 2:   Chapter 21
  Day 3:   Chapter 22
           Chapter 23, Section 1
  Day 4:   Chapter 23, Sections 2-3
  Day 5:   Chapter 23, Sections 4-7

Chapter 1: The Divine Dilemma and the Gospel

In the Scriptures, we learn that God is holy; righteous; and deserving of all love, reverence, and obedience. We also learn that man, though created good, has corrupted himself, defied God's law, and exposed himself to divine judgment. In this study, we will discover the marvelous work of God to reconcile fallen man to Himself.

THE DIVINE DILEMMA

The word "dilemma" is defined by Webster's Dictionary as "a situation involving a choice between equally unsatisfactory alternatives" or "a problem seemingly incapable of a satisfactory solution." In the Scriptures, the greatest of all dilemmas is set before us: God is righteous; therefore, He must act according to the strictest rules of justice, acquitting the innocent and condemning the guilty. If He pardons the guilty and does not punish every infraction of His law and every act of disobedience, then He is unjust. However, if He does act with justice toward every man—if He gives to every man exactly what he deserves—then all men will be condemned. How can God be just and yet show mercy to those who ought to be condemned? To rephrase the words of the Apostle Paul in Romans 3:26 as a question:

How can God be just and the justifier of sinful men?

WHY CAN'T GOD JUST FORGIVE?

A person might ask, "Why can't God simply forgive man's sin and be done with it? The Scriptures command us to freely forgive, so why would it be wrong for God to do the same?" The answer to this question is three-fold.

First, God is not like us, but is of infinitely greater worth than all of His creation combined. Therefore, it is not only right but also necessary for Him to both seek His own glory and defend it. Because of who He is, even the slightest form of rebellion is a grotesque offense to His person, a crime of highest treason, and worthy of the strictest censure. For Him to allow any offense against His person to go unpunished would be a two-fold injustice: (1) He would do injustice to His own person by denying Himself the glory that rightfully belongs to Him as God; and (2) He would do injustice to His creation by allowing it to deny the very reason for its own existence (*i.e.* the glory of God) and to run headlong into futility. If this is too difficult for modern man to accept, it is only because he has such a low view of God.

Second, God cannot simply forgive man's sin and be done with it because there are no contradictions in His character. The Scriptures teach that God is perfect (without contradiction) in all His attributes and works. Therefore, He will always act in a way that is perfectly consistent with all that He is. He will not exalt one attribute at the expense of another, nor will He deny one aspect of His character in order to manifest another. He is loving, compassionate, and longsuffering; however, He is also holy, righteous, and just in all His works and judgments. He cannot deny His holiness in the name of love, and He cannot ignore His justice in order to exercise mercy. Many well-intentioned evangelists have wrongly taught that instead of being just with sinful man, God has determined to be loving. However, the logical conclusion to this untruth is that God's love is unjust or that He is able to turn His back on His own justice in the name of love. Such a statement betrays an ignorance of God's attributes. The marvel of the gospel is not that God chose love over justice, but that He was able to remain just while granting forgiveness in love.

Third, God is the Judge of all the earth. It is His place to see that justice is done, that evil is punished, and that right is vindicated. It would not be appropriate for the heavenly Judge to pardon the wicked any more than it would be for an earthly judge to pardon the guilty criminal who stands before him in a court of law. Is it not the frequent complaint of many that our justice system is corrupt? Do we not cringe when convicted criminals are pardoned? Should we expect less justice from God than we do from our own judges? It is a well-founded truth that without the enforcement of justice, all nations, peoples, and cultures would run headlong into anarchy and self-destruction. If God ignored His own righteousness; if pardon were granted without the satisfaction of justice; and if there were no final judgment of evil, creation could not bear it.

THE DILEMMA SET FORTH IN THE SCRIPTURES

Possibly the greatest question in all the Scriptures is: "How can God be just and yet show mercy to those who ought to be condemned?" How can He be just and the justifier of sinful men? In the following Scriptures, this **divine dilemma** will appear with undeniable clarity.

1. In Exodus 23:7 and Romans 4:5, we find excellent examples of the divine dilemma—how can God be just and yet justify the wicked?

    a. *What does God declare about Himself in Exodus 23:7?*

       (1) I will not A_____ the G_____.

          NOTES: The word "acquit" comes from the Hebrew word **tsadeq**, which means, "to justify, vindicate, or declare right."

    b. *How does the Apostle Paul describe God in Romans 4:5?*

       (1) He who J_____ the U_____.

          NOTES: The word "justifies" comes from the Greek verb **dikaióō**, which means, "to declare right or acquit."

    c. *How do these two texts together illustrate the divine dilemma?*

       _____

       _____

       _____

_____

_____

_____

NOTES: Exodus 23:7 clearly affirms that God will not acquit or justify the guilty, but will act with perfect justice toward him. However, in Romans 4:5, the Scriptures boldly declare the great hope of every believer to be that God justifies the ungodly! How can both statements be true?

2. In Proverbs 17:15 is found one of the most powerful illustrations in all of the Scriptures regarding the divine dilemma.

   a. _What universal and immutable truth is set forth in Proverbs 17:15?_

      (1) He who J_____ the W_____ is an

      A_____ to the Lord.

      NOTES: The word "abomination" comes from the Hebrew word **tow`ebah**, which denotes something that is abominable, disgusting, or loathsome. It is one of the strongest words in the Hebrew Scriptures!

   b. _How do the truth revealed in Proverbs 17:15 and the truth that God justifies the ungodly (Romans 4:5) illustrate the divine dilemma?_

_____

_____

_____

_____

_____

_____

NOTES: We have previously stated the divine dilemma in the rephrased words of the Apostle Paul: "How can God be just and the justifier of the wicked?" Here the dilemma is restated: "How can God justify the wicked in a way that is not abominable or detestable to His holy and righteous character?"

3. In Exodus 34:5-7 is found still another clear example of the divine dilemma. Read the text, and complete the exercises.

    a. *In verse 7, God makes two seemingly contradictory declarations which powerfully illustrate the divine dilemma. Identify these declarations.*

        (1) God forgives I_____, T_____, and S_____.

        (2) God will by no means leave the G_____ U_____.

    b. *Explain the dilemma that is illustrated in verse 7.*

        _____

        _____

        _____

        _____

        _____

    > **NOTES:** How can both statements be true? The same Scripture that promises pardon for all kinds of sin warns that God will not forgive the guilty or leave him unpunished.

4. To bring this chapter of our study to a close, we will consider one of the most beautiful passages in the entire Bible. In Romans 4:7-8, the Apostle Paul quotes from Psalm 32:1-2. Read over the passage in Romans until you are familiar with its contents, and then answer the following questions.

    a. *According to Romans 4:7-8, what are the three characteristics of the man who is blessed before God?*

        (1) His L_____ deeds have been F_____ (v.7).

        (2) His S_____ have been C_____ (v.7).

        (3) His S_____ the Lord will **not** take into A_____ (v.8).

    b. *What theological difficulties are presented in Romans 4:7-8?*

        _____

        _____

        _____

NOTES: How can a just God forgive a man's lawless deeds, cover his sin, and not take it into account?

THE DIVINE ANSWER

One of the greatest affirmations of Scripture is that nothing is impossible for God! This truth is most clearly revealed in the manner which God contrived to maintain His righteous character while pardoning sinful men: God became a Man, bore the sins of His people upon the cross, and suffered the divine judgment that was decreed against them. By His suffering and death in the place of His people, God satisfied the demands of His own justice against them and appeased His own wrath toward them so that His mercy toward them might be perfectly consistent with His righteousness.

The grand dilemma—"How can God be just and yet justify the wicked?"—has now been answered in the gospel of Jesus Christ. The same God who in righteousness condemns the wicked became a Man and died in the place of the wicked. God does not ignore, forego, or pervert the demands of His justice in order to justify the wicked; rather, He paid the demands of justice through the suffering and death of the Son of God on Calvary.

_____

_____

_____

_____

2. Hebrews 12:2 clearly teaches that the motivation which led Christ to Calvary's cross was the joy that was set before Him. However, we must ask ourselves: of what did that joy consist? What do the following texts teach us?

    a. *THE JOY OF RETURNING TO HIS FATHER'S PRESENCE (PSALM 16:9-11)*

    _____

    _____

    _____

    _____

    _____

    _____

    NOTES: The Apostle Peter quotes this text in his sermon on the Day of Pentecost as a reference to Christ's resurrection and exaltation (Acts 2:25-28), and the Apostle Paul makes reference to it in his sermon in the synagogue in Antioch (Acts 13:35). It was an immense trial for the Son of God to leave His Father's dwelling place in heaven, but it was an infinitely greater trial to bear the sin of His people and to suffer in their place. He endured such indescribable agonies, even despised them, because He looked forward to the future hope of once again dwelling with His Father and rejoicing in His presence.

    b. *THE JOY OF SHARING IN HIS FATHER'S GLORY (JOHN 17:4-5, 24)*

    _____

    _____

    _____

    _____

_____

_____

NOTES: Part of the joy that moved Christ to offer Himself for the sins of His people was His future glorification or exaltation to the place that was rightfully His even before the foundation of the world. He would return as Lord and Savior—the exalted Victor who overcame every obstacle to obtain the redemption of His people.

c. ***THE JOY OF GAINING FOR HIMSELF A REDEEMED PEOPLE*** – Before the foundation of the world, God ordained to save a people out of the multitude of sinful humanity, that they might live for the glory, honor, and praise of the Son. In accordance with the will of the Father and in view of this joy set before Him—the joy of redeeming a people of His very own—the Son willingly, even joyfully, endured all for the sake of His Bride and for the joy that she would ultimately bring Him. Through His incarnation and death, He has secured a great congregation for Himself from every tribe, tongue, people, and nation. He has made them to be a source of continuous joy, satisfaction, and glory throughout all of eternity. What do the following texts teach regarding this truth?

(1) Psalm 2:8

_____

_____

_____

_____

_____

(2) Isaiah 53:11

_____

_____

_____

_____

_____

(3) Luke 15:10

_____

_____

_____

_____

(4) Hebrews 2:11-13

_____

_____

_____

_____

(5) Revelation 5:9-10; 7:9-10; 22:3-5

_____

_____

_____

_____

Chapter 4: The Son of God in Glory

To understand the magnitude and majesty of the coming of the Son of God, we must first consider both His divine nature and His eternal glory. In this chapter, we will learn that the Son of God did not begin to exist at His birth in Bethlehem; rather, He has existed throughout eternity, sharing equality with God the Father in both nature and glory. It was not a mere man or even an archangel that gave his life for our redemption; it was the eternal Son of God—the Creator, Sustainer, and Sovereign Lord of all. Only to the degree that we have a proper view of the Son will we have a high view of the gospel and an appreciation for it.

THE SON'S DEITY

The Scriptures testify that the one true God exists as a Trinity (from the Latin word **trinitas**, which means, "threefold" or "three in one"): the Father, the Son, and the Holy Spirit. They are three distinct Persons, who are distinguishable from one another; yet they share the same divine **nature** or **essence** and relate to one another in eternal and unbroken fellowship. The Son, who became a Man and died upon the cross of Calvary, is the eternal God: equal to the Father and the Spirit in every way and sharing in their incomprehensible glory.

It is absolutely essential that we comprehend the importance of the teaching before us. The deity of the Son of God is a fundamental doctrine of the Christian faith. Any view that sees Him as inferior to the Father or as a "god of lesser glory" is simply not Christian. The Son is not a created being, He is not an angel, and He is not a demigod to be ranked somewhere between God and creation. He is God in the highest sense of the term. The assurance of our salvation and the fidelity of our gospel depend upon our reverent and wholehearted acceptance of this truth.

1. In John 1:1-4 is found one of the clearest declarations of both the deity and eternality of the Son of God. Identify the truths that are revealed in this text.

    a. *In the B_____ was the W_____ (v.1)*. This is a clear reference to the Son of God (v.14). "Word" is translated from the Greek word **lógos**, which means, "word" or "reason." The Jews often used this term in reference to God. To the Greeks, it denoted the divine reason or rational principle that governed the universe. When applied to the Son, it communicates that He is deity (fully and truly God) and the Mediator through whom God reveals Himself to His creation. The Son was "in the beginning" with God before creation and is uncreated, eternal, and divine.

    b. *And the Word was W_____ God (v.1)*. This is a reference to the relationship of unity yet distinction that existed between the Father and the Son throughout eternity. Firstly, it denotes unity and equality—the Father and the Son existed in perfect fellowship. The phrase could be translated, "And the Word was face to face with God," denoting the intimate fellowship, communion, and delight that existed among the Father, Son, and Holy Spirit. Second, it denotes distinction—the Father and the Son are of the same divine essence, but They are two real and distinct Persons who exist in perfect fellowship together with the Holy Spirit.

c. *And the Word W_____ G_____ (v.1).* This is an undeniable declaration of the Word's deity. In the original Greek, the phrase is literally, "and God was the Word" (**kaí Theós ên ho Lógos**). The predicate nominative (God) precedes the subject (the Word) in order to emphasize the fact that the Word was really and truly God. The Son of God is God the Son. The fullness of deity dwells in Him (Colossians 2:9).

d. *All things came into being T_____ Him, and apart from Him nothing came into being that has come into being (v.3).* Positively, all things were created through the Son (see also Colossians 1:16). He was the co-agent of creation along with the Father and the Spirit. Negatively, nothing exists that did not come into being through Him. The Son was not only in the beginning with God, but He was also doing the works of God as God.

e. *I_____ Him was L_____, and the life was the Light of men (v.4).* Psalm 36:9 declares, "For with You [*i.e.* God] is the fountain of life; in Your light we see light." It is remarkable that what the Psalmist ascribes to God, the Apostle John ascribes to the Son. Everything that has ever lived and moved has done so by the grace of the Son of God. Any true knowledge of God that men have ever possessed came to them as a gracious endowment from the Son. It is an incomprehensible marvel that the Fountain of all life would lay down His life for the lifeless.

2. In Philippians 2:6, we find still another proof of Christ's deity and eternality. Identify the truths that are revealed in this text.

   a. *Although He E_____ in the F_____ of God.* The Son did not begin to exist at His incarnation; He is eternal, without beginning or end. The word "form" comes from the Greek word **morphê**, which refers not only to the outward or external appearance of a person but also to his or her essential character or underlying reality. The Son did not merely **seem** to be God in appearance; rather, He **was** God in essence or nature.

   b. *He did not regard E_____ with God a thing to be grasped.* The word "equality" comes from the Greek word **ísos**, which means, "to be equal in quantity or quality." In the Son, all the fullness (quantity) of deity (quality) dwelled (Colossians 2:9). He lacked nothing with respect to deity, but was equal in every way to the fullest meaning of the term.

THE SON'S GLORY

Having affirmed the eternal existence and deity of the Son of God, we will now concern ourselves with the glory that was His before the incarnation, before the foundation of the world, even from all eternity. Although the Scriptures give us only glimpses of eternity past, it is enough to prove that the Son was "God" in the highest and most exalted sense of the word and that He bore the glory of God as God. He was with the Father and shared His Father's glory (John 17:5). He was His Father's supreme and unending delight, and it was the Father's good pleasure that He be the instrument and epicenter of creation—the source of its joy, the object of its worship, and the great purpose or end of its existence. Since the dawn of creation, every sublime being that dwells in heaven has had only one great desire—to gaze upon the glory of God in the face of His exalted Son! It is only when we understand something of these truths that we can have a proper view of and appreciation for the gospel. It was not a mere man or even an angel that robed himself in flesh and died for us on that day. It was the God of Glory, the Lord of the universe, the Object of all worship, and the One through whom all things were made and for whom all things exist!

1. In Colossians 1:15-17 is found a powerful declaration of the Son's eternal nature and the glory that He shared with the Father from before His incarnation. Based upon the text, complete each of the following declarations.

   a. *The Son is the I_____ of the invisible God (v.15).* This word comes from the Greek word **eikôn**, which refers to an "image" or "likeness." Only God can bear the exact likeness of God. Hebrews 1:3 declares, "He is the radiance of His glory and the exact representation of His nature."

   b. *The Son is the F_____ of all creation (v.15).* This is neither a denial of Christ's deity nor evidence that He is a created being. In Psalm 89:27, God declares the following concerning David: "I also shall make him My firstborn, the highest of the kings of the earth." It is clear that David was the "firstborn" of God only in the sense that he was ranked above all other kings. The Son of God is "firstborn" in the sense that He is exalted above all creation and is distinct from it. To Him belong all the rights and privileges of a firstborn son.

   c. *The Son is B_____ all things (v.17).* The Son's eternality, supremacy, and preeminence are communicated in this declaration.

   d. *The Son is the C_____ of all things (v.16).* All creation owes its existence to the Son, is directly related to Him, and stands in relation to Him.

   e. *The Son is the Sustainer of all things—in Him all things H_____ together (v.17).* All creation exists in utter and total dependence upon the Son. He "upholds all things by the word of His power" (Hebrews 1:3). The Son is not like the mythological Atlas, who groans under the weight of a single world; on the contrary, He upholds countless worlds with the ease of a single word!

   f. *The Son is the Great End of all things—all things were created F_____ Him (v.16).* The eternal glory of the Son is seen in the fact that all things were made **through** Him and **for** His glory and good pleasure.

2. In Isaiah 6:1-10 is recorded one of Scripture's most graphic and majestic portrayals of God and His glory; however, with further investigation we discover that Isaiah's vision of God was a vision of the Son! Read through Isaiah 6:1-5 until you are familiar with its contents, and then answer the following questions.

   a. *According to verses 1-3, Isaiah saw the L_____.*

   NOTES: In verse one, the title "Lord" is translated from the Hebrew word **adonay**; but in verse three, it is translated from the Hebrew word **Yahweh** or **Jehovah**. The One

Isaiah sees is unquestionably God; however, John 12:39-41 identifies this Being as the *second* Person of the Trinity, the Son of God, thus affirming Christ as God.

b. *According to Isaiah verse 1, how is the Son of God described? What does this tell us of His glory?*

_____

_____

_____

_____

_____

NOTES: The Son is described as lifted up above all creation in heaven and on earth. The train of His robe filling the temple represents His universal, unlimited, and unhindered sovereignty.

c. *According to verses 2-3, what is the response of the seraphim (possibly the highest ranking beings in creation) to the Son of God? What does this teach us about His glory and preeminence?*

_____

_____

_____

_____

_____

_____

NOTES: The most powerful and majestic creatures in the universe bow with reverence in the presence of the Son of God. The word "holy" comes from the Hebrew word

_____

_____

NOTES: It is one thing for a rich man to take upon himself a vow of poverty and walk among the poor. It is quite another thing for the very God of the universe to take on flesh and live among the lowliest of men as one of them. We must remember that there was a definite and certain redemptive purpose in the Son's self-imposed poverty—He left the glories of heaven so that we might enter in.

6. In I Timothy 3:16 is found one of the most concise and beautiful statements in all the Scriptures regarding the incarnation. What does the Apostle Paul declare about the incarnation in the first phrase of this text?

   a. *By common confession, G_____ is the M_____ of godliness.* The phrase, "by common confession," may also be translated, "by consent of all" or "without controversy or dispute." The word "mystery" [Greek: ***mustêrion***] refers to that which is or has been hidden or unintelligible. The word "godliness" [Greek: ***eusébeia***] refers to all true devotion toward God. This phrase is best understood as: "All Christians confess without dispute that great is the mystery which is the foundation and source of all true devotion to God."

   b. *He who was R_____ in the F_____.* The mystery that is the foundation and source of all true godliness is the Son of God and the saving work that He accomplished "in the flesh." The incarnation is a fundamental doctrine of the Christian faith. If Jesus was not conceived both **of the Holy Spirit** and **in the womb a virgin**, then He was not God incarnate, and the rest of the gospel is a lie—the cross has no saving power; the resurrection was a hoax; and we remain in our sins, separated from God and without hope.

Chapter 7: The Son Lived a Perfect Life

It was not enough for the Son of God to become a Man; it was required that He live a life of perfect obedience under the law of God. If He had been found guilty of even one violation of the law in thought, disposition, word, or deed; He would have disqualified Himself as a sacrifice for sin. For this reason, it is correct to say that without Christ's perfect obedience throughout the full course of His life, all other aspects of His life and ministry would be of no effect. Only a perfectly obedient Second Adam could undo what the first Adam caused by his moral failure (Romans 5:12-19). Only a Lamb unblemished and spotless could give His life for the sins of the world (John 1:29; I Peter 1:19). Only the just could give Himself for the unjust that He might bring them to God (I Peter 3:18). Only a sinless Savior could give His life as a ransom for many (Mark 10:45).

1. Before we advance any further, we must consider Romans 8:3. What does it teach us about Christ's incarnation?

_____

_____

_____

NOTES: In the incarnation, the Son of God did not take upon Himself the body of pre-fall mankind; rather, He took a body that, though untainted by sin, was subject to all the terrible consequences of our fallen race. As a Man, He was subject to the same limitations, frailties, afflictions, and anguish of fallen humanity. It would have been a great humiliation if He had taken the nature of humanity before the fall, when it was in its full glory and strength. However, He was sent in the "likeness of sinful flesh"!

2. According to Luke 1:35, how is it that Jesus was conceived without the depraved Adamic nature that has led to the moral ruin of the rest of the human race?

_____

_____

_____

NOTES: The word "holy" is the same word used of the Spirit. He was the "Holy Child" because He was conceived of the "Holy Spirit."

3. In Scripture, a person's name has great significance in that it often describes who he is and reveals something about his character. What is the name given to the Christ in Acts 3:14, and what does it teach us about His nature?

   a. *The* H_____ *and* R_____ *One.*

   NOTES: Peter is quoting from Psalm 16:10. The word "holy" [Greek: *hágios*] refers to one who is undefiled by sin, free from wickedness, and morally pure. The word "righteous" [Greek: *díkaios*] denotes conformity to the nature and will of God. It is significant that this title, which is ascribed uniquely to God in the Old Testament (Isaiah 24:16), is ascribed to Jesus three times in the book of Acts (Acts 3:14; 7:52; 22:14).

4. What does the Father testify concerning Jesus in Matthew 3:17? What does His testimony communicate to us about Christ's nature and deeds?

   _____

   _____

   _____

   _____

   NOTES: This declaration is first found in the Messianic prophecy recorded in Isaiah 42:1. It was declared at Christ's baptism (Matthew 3:17; Mark 1:11; Luke 3:22) and transfiguration (Matthew 17:5; Mark 9:7). God's testimony concerning Christ proves His sinlessness. The Most Holy can only delight in the Most Holy. The slightest sin would have turned God's smile to a frown.

5. According to the following texts, what did Jesus testify concerning Himself and His obedience to the will of God?

   a. *John 8:29*

   _____

   _____

   _____

NOTES: The most amazing aspect of Christ's claim is the adverb "always." Fallen man cannot even make a claim to periodic perfect obedience, but Christ claims an obedience that is not only perfect but also perpetual or unbroken. He was obedient, without even the slightest flaw, throughout the entire course of His life.

b. *John 17:4*

_____

_____

_____

_____

NOTES: To claim perfection before men is a bold thing, but to do the same before God is quite another. With full and unflinching confidence, Jesus stands before the Father and claims perfect obedience in heart and deed. The best of God's servants among men cannot make the claim that Jesus made, but must admit, "We are unworthy slaves; we have done only that which we ought to have done" (Luke 17:10).

6. According to the Gospel accounts, even those who most opposed Christ were forced to recognize His righteousness. What do the following texts teach about this truth?

_____ *Matthew 27:3-4*   a. *The thief saw that Christ had done nothing wrong.*

_____ *Matthew 27:19*   b. *Pilate's wife called Christ a righteous man.*

_____ *Matthew 27:23-24; Luke 23:4*   c. *Judas recognized Christ's innocence.*

_____ *Luke 23:39-41*   d. *The centurion testified that Christ was innocent.*

_____ *Luke 23:47*   e. *Pilate found no guilt in Christ.*

7. In the following, we will consider some of the most important texts in the Epistles regarding the sinlessness of Jesus. Summarize each text in your own words.

a. *II Corinthians 5:21*

_____

_____

_____

_____

_____

b. *Hebrews 4:15*

_____

_____

_____

_____

NOTES: Jesus was tempted in all things common to our frail human condition. In our weakness, we usually fall before lesser temptations, and we are therefore rarely confronted with greater ones. Christ prevailed over the lesser temptations common to all **and** over the greatest that no other man has ever faced.

c. *Hebrews 7:26*

_____

_____

_____

_____

NOTES: The word "holy" [Greek: ***hósios***] indicates the state of one who is undefiled by sin, free from evil, and morally pure. The word "innocent" or "harmless" [Greek: ***ákakos***] refers to one who is innocent of destructive evil or malice. The word "undefiled" [Greek: ***amíantos***] can also be translated, "unsoiled" or "unstained." The phrase, "separated from sinners," refers to the great distinction between Christ and mankind—He was without sin.

d. *I Peter 1:19*

_____

_____

_____

_____

NOTES: Christ's blood was precious because He was the Lamb unblemished and spotless. The word "unblemished" [Greek: *ámōmos*] denotes that which is faultless or without blame. The word "spotless" [Greek: *áspilos*] denotes that which is without spot, unsullied or unstained, free from censure or reproach. According to the law, the sacrificial lamb had to be free from all defect (Leviticus 22:20-25; Numbers 6:14; 28:3, 9). Thus the Christ had to be free from all sin.

e. *I Peter 2:22*

_____

_____

_____

_____

NOTES: This entire verse is taken from the Messianic prophecy found in the Septuagint's version of Isaiah 53:9. It is a strong and clear declaration of the sinless perfection of the Lord Jesus Christ. In Scripture, the mouth or speech of an individual is an indicator of the condition of the heart (Isaiah 6:5; Matthew 15:18). Christ's speech was without deceit because His heart was without deceit. James writes, "If anyone does not stumble in what he says, he is a perfect man, able to bridle the whole body as well" (James 3:2). The logic is simple: Jesus did not stumble in what He said because He was perfect.

f. *I John 3:5*

_____

_____

_____

_____

NOTES: Christ knew no sin (II Corinthians 5:21), and in Him there was no sin (I John 3:5).

Chapter 8: The Son Bore Our Sin

The cross of Christ brings to mind the insults and physical pain He suffered. To die on a cross was the worst of all humiliations and tortures. Nevertheless, the physical pain and shame heaped upon Christ by men were not the most important aspects of the cross. We are saved not merely because men beat him with whips and nailed Him to a cross. We are saved because He bore our sin and was crushed under God's judgment.

THE SON STOOD IN OUR PLACE

The purpose of the Son's incarnation and His perfect life is found in the biblical truth that He came to be the substitution for His people. He came to bear their guilt, to stand in their place of judgment, and to suffer their penalty of death. This is one of the greatest themes of the Scriptures and a foundation stone of the Christian faith. For this reason the work of Christ is often called **vicarious**. The word "vicarious" comes from the Latin word **vicarius** [**vicis** = change, alternation, or stead] and denotes the act of changing places or standing in the stead of another as a substitution.

CHRIST DIED "IN PLACE OF" HIS PEOPLE

The Greek preposition **anti** is employed with regard to the death of Christ on the cross for His people.[1] The preposition means, "instead of" or "in place of."

> But when he heard that Archelaus was reigning over Judea **in place of** his father Herod, he was afraid to go there. Then after being warned by God in a dream, he left for the regions of Galilee... (Matthew 2:22)

> Just as the Son of Man did not come to be served, but to serve, and to give His life a ransom **for** many. (Matthew 20:28)

CHRIST DIED "FOR" HIS PEOPLE

The Greek preposition **peri** is employed with regard to the death of Christ on the cross for His people.[2] The preposition is often translated as "for."

> For this is My blood of the covenant, which is poured out **for** many for forgiveness of sins. (Matthew 26:28)

> In this is love, not that we loved God, but that He loved us and sent His Son to be the propitiation **for** our sins. (I John 4:10)

---

[1] See also Mark 10:45 for another example of the use of this preposition.
[2] See also I John 2:2 for another example of the use of this preposition.

_____

_____

_____

_____

NOTES: Since it was impossible for a single offering to fully typify or illustrate the twofold purpose of the Messiah's atoning death, an offering involving two sacrificial goats was put before the people (Leviticus 16:5-10). The first goat was slain as a sin offering before the Lord, and its blood was sprinkled on and in front of the Mercy Seat, behind the veil in the Holy of Holies (vv.9, 15, 20). It is a wonderful illustration of Christ's death as a propitiation—He shed His blood to satisfy the justice of God, appease His wrath, and bring peace. The second goat was presented before the Lord as the scapegoat (v.10). Upon the head of this animal, the High Priest laid "both of his hands...and confess[ed] over it all the iniquities of the sons of Israel and all their transgressions in regard to all their sins" (v.21). The scapegoat was then sent away into the wilderness, bearing on itself all the iniquities of the people into a solitary land (vv.21-22). It typified Christ, who "bore our sins in His body on the cross" (I Peter 2:24) and suffered and died alone "outside the camp" (Hebrews 13:11-12). It is a wonderful illustration of Christ's death as an expiation—He carried away our sin. The psalmist wrote, "As far as the east is from the west, so far has He removed our transgressions from us" (Psalm 103:12).

2. The sacrifices in the Old Testament were only shadows or types that pointed to and found their ultimate fulfillment in Christ. He is the great Sin-Bearer who offered His life for our sins. What do the following Scriptures teach us about this truth?

   a. _Isaiah 53:6_

   _____

   _____

   _____

   _____

   _____

   NOTES: The Lord [Hebrew: **Yahweh**] imputed the sins of His people to His only begotten Son. The word "fall" indicates falling upon or striking. The sins of God's people fell upon the Christ with an overwhelming, rushing violence, as an attacking army or a sudden and relentless storm (see also Isaiah 53:11-12).

b. *II Corinthians 5:21*

_____

_____

_____

_____

_____

NOTES: Christ was made sin in the same way that the believer is made "the righteousness of God." The moment a person believes in Jesus, he is pardoned of his sin, and the righteousness of Christ is imputed to him or placed in his account. God legally declares the believer to be righteous and treats him as righteous. When Christ hung upon the cross, He did not actually become corrupt or unrighteous; but God imputed our sins to Him, legally declared Him to be guilty, and treated Him as guilty.

c. *Hebrews 9:27-28*

_____

_____

_____

_____

_____

NOTES: The purpose of Christ's incarnation and death was that He might bear the sins of His people. The word "bear" comes from the Greek word ***anaphérō***, which means literally, "to lift up."

d. *I Peter 2:24*

_____

_____

_____

_____

_____

NOTES: The word "bore" comes from the Greek word **_anaphérō_**, which means literally, "to lift up." The cross was the cruelest instrument of torture ever conceived by depraved humanity, yet this was the altar upon which the Son of God made His sacrifice. The purpose of Christ's death on the cross was not only to restore us to a right relationship with God, but also to enable us by the power of God to die to sin and live to righteousness. Peter quotes Isaiah 53:5, not with reference to physical healing, but to healing from sin and its consequences.

3. To conclude this section, we will consider John 3:14-15, a very important passage. What does this text teach us about Christ bearing the sins of His people?

_____

_____

_____

_____

_____

_____

NOTES: Jesus' words must be understood in the context of Numbers 21:5-9. Because of Israel's nearly constant rebellion against the Lord and their rejection of His gracious provisions, God sent "fiery serpents" among the people, and many died. However, as a result of the people's repentance and Moses' intercession, God once again made provision for their salvation. He commanded Moses to "make a fiery serpent, and set it on a standard." He then promised that each person who was bitten, when he looked at this bronze serpent, would live. The narrative provides a powerful picture of the cross. The Israelites were dying from the venom of the fiery serpents; men die from the venom of their own sin. Moses was commanded to place the cause of death high upon a pole; God placed the cause of our death upon His own Son as He hung high upon a cross. He had come "in the likeness of sinful flesh" (Romans 8:3) and was made "to be sin on our behalf" (II Corinthians 5:21). The Israelite who believed God and looked upon the brazen serpent would live; the man who believes God's testimony concerning His Son and looks upon Him with faith will be saved (I John 5:10-11).

Chapter 9: The Son Became a Curse

In the preceding lesson, we learned that Christ was "made sin" on our behalf. In this lesson, we will consider the equally incomprehensible doctrine that Christ became a curse for us. The Scriptures clearly teach that all who have sinned are under the curse of the law. To save us, the Son of God became a Man, bore our guilt, and became a curse in our place.

1. What does Galatians 3:10 teach us about sinful, fallen man's position before God?

_____

_____

_____

_____

_____

NOTES: The phrase, "For as many as are of the works of the Law," is a reference to those who are depending upon their own moral virtue, personal righteousness, or obedience to the law of God to make them acceptable before God. The Scriptures declare that all such individuals are under a curse because the law requires a perfect and unbroken obedience that no man has ever accomplished. The word "curse" comes from the Greek word **katára**, which may also be translated, "imprecation," "malediction," or "execration." It denotes a violent denouncing of something or someone with intense disgust, loathing, or hatred. From heaven's perspective, those who break God's law are vile and worthy of all loathing; they are justly exposed to divine vengeance and devoted to eternal destruction. Although such language is offensive to the world and even to many who consider themselves to be Christians, it is biblical language, and it must be stated. If for etiquette's sake we refuse to explain and illustrate these hard truths of Scripture, then God will not be held as holy, men will not understand their dreadful predicament, and the price paid by Christ will never be truly appreciated. Unless we comprehend what it means for man to be under the divine curse, we will never comprehend what it meant for Christ to "become a curse for us." We will never fully understand the horror and beauty of what was done for us on Calvary!

2. According to Galatians 3:13, what has Christ done to redeem us from the curse?

_____

_____

c. *Christy was R*_____ *on the third day according to the Scriptures (v.4).* The resurrection of Jesus Christ should never be tacked on to the end of our gospel presentation as though it were an afterthought or a nonessential. In the book of Acts, the proclamation of the resurrection is given priority!

3. All four Gospel writers are careful to narrate the death of Jesus. Even though their descriptions are concise, they are nonetheless certain. Read each of the following accounts: Matthew 27:50; Mark 15:37; Luke 23:46; John 19:30. What are some of the major thoughts communicated?

_____

_____

_____

_____

NOTES: In the Gospel accounts, there are two things that are being communicated: (1) the reality of Christ's death—the wages of sin is death, and Christ paid that penalty for His people by dying in their place—and (2) Christ's sovereignty over His death—He yielded or gave up His spirit (Matthew 27:50; John 19:30); He committed His spirit into the hands of His Father (Luke 23:46). Christ did not die as an unwilling martyr; rather, He willingly gave His life as an atoning sacrifice in His people's place.

4. The following verses are some of the most important in Scripture with regard to Christ's death and its significance for His people. Summarize the meaning of each text in your own words.

a. *Romans 5:6*

_____

_____

_____

_____

b. *Romans 5:8*

_____

_____

_____

_____

  c. *Romans 5:10*

_____

_____

_____

_____

5. According to II Corinthians 5:14-15, how should we as believers respond to Christ's death on our behalf?

_____

_____

_____

_____

_____

6. We will conclude this lesson with a view of heaven and eternity. According to Revelation 5:8-10, what will be the great song of angels and the redeemed throughout all the ages?

_____

_____

_____

_____

_____

CHRIST DIED "ON BEHALF OF" HIS PEOPLE

The Greek preposition **hupér** (or **hypér**) is employed with regard to the death of Christ on the cross for His people.[3] The preposition means, "on behalf of."

> I am the good shepherd; the good shepherd lays down His life **for** the sheep. (John 10:11)

> And He died **for** all, so that they who live might no longer live for themselves, but for Him who died and rose again **on their behalf**. (II Corinthians 5:15)

> For Christ also died for sins once for all, the just **for** the unjust... (I Peter 3:18)

CHRIST DIED "FOR THE SAKE OF" HIS PEOPLE

The Greek preposition **diá** is employed with regard to the death of Christ on the cross for His people. The preposition means, "for the sake of" or "because of."

> For through your knowledge he who is weak is ruined, the brother **for whose sake** Christ died. (I Corinthians 8:11)

> For you know the grace of our Lord Jesus Christ, that though He was rich, yet **for your sake** He became poor, so that you through His poverty might become rich. (II Corinthians 8:9)

THE SON BORE OUR SIN

In the Scriptures, we learn about the **imputation** of Adam's sin to the entire human race. In God's perfect righteousness and inscrutable wisdom, He considered the sin of Adam to be the sin of all; therefore, all men sinned **in Adam** and are considered guilty of Adam's sin. In the following pages, we will consider another aspect of imputation—the imputation of our sin to Christ. As Adam's sin was imputed to all mankind, so the sins of God's people were imputed to Christ.

1. In the Old Testament, the sacrificing of animals in the place of God's people was only a shadow or type that pointed to and found its ultimate fulfillment in Christ. Nevertheless, these animal sacrifices provide an excellent illustration of how Christ bore the sins of God's people and offered His own life as a sacrifice in their place. Read Leviticus 16:21-22; explain how it relates to the sacrifice of Christ.

_____

_____

---

[3] See also Mark 14:24; Romans 5:6, 8; Galatians 3:13; Ephesians 5:2; I Timothy 2:6; Titus 2:14; and I John 3:16 for more examples of the use of this preposition.

Chapter 12: Christ Our Propitiation

The word "propitiation" comes from the Latin verb **propiciare**, which means, "to propitiate, appease, or make favorable." In the English New Testament, the word "propitiation" is translated from the Greek word **hilasmós**, which refers to a sacrifice that satisfies the demands of God's justice and appeases His wrath. To fully understand the meaning and significance of propitiation, we will review some of the central truths we have already learned in previous chapters.

In the Scriptures, the greatest of all dilemmas is set before us: God is righteous; therefore, He must act according to the strictest rules of justice, acquitting the innocent and condemning the guilty. If He pardons the guilty and does not punish every infraction of the law and every act of disobedience, then He is unjust. However, if He does act with justice toward every man and gives to every man exactly what he deserves, then all men will be condemned. This brings us to one of the greatest questions in all the Scriptures: "How can God be just and yet show mercy to those who ought to be condemned?" Or, as we previously rephrased the words of the Apostle Paul in Romans 3:26, "How can God be just and the justifier of sinful men?"

The answer to these questions is found in the word "propitiation" as it relates to the gospel of Jesus Christ. The same God who in righteousness condemns the wicked became a Man and died in place of the wicked. God did not ignore, forego, or pervert the demands of His justice in order to justify the wicked; but He satisfied the demands of divine justice against them and appeased His own wrath through the suffering and death of His Son. Christ is our propitiation in that His sacrifice has made it possible for a holy and just God to be merciful toward us and pardon our offenses against Him.

FORENSIC OR PENAL SATISFACTION

Whenever reference is made to Christ's satisfaction of the demands of divine justice, it is important to understand exactly what is meant. Basically, there are two types of satisfaction: **commercial** and **forensic** (also called **penal**).

> **Commercial Satisfaction:** The debt is satisfied only when the exact amount is paid. A debt of $50 is not satisfied by a payment of $25, nor can a debt of ten ounces of gold be satisfied with a payment of the same weight in clay.

> **Forensic or Penal Satisfaction:** The debt is satisfied when the criminal serves the sentence decreed by the judge. The sentence is not required to be of the same nature as the crime. All that is required is that it should be a just equivalent. For theft, it may be a fine; for murder, imprisonment; and for treason, banishment.

From the above illustrations, it is evident that Christ's sufferings were not commercial, but **forensic** or **penal** in nature. Christ did not pay the exact penalty under which His people were condemned—He did not suffer eternal condemnation in hell. But His sufferings were exactly what a holy and just God determined should be paid in order to satisfy divine justice and release the guilty from the penalty of sin.

SATISFACTION AND CHRIST'S INFINITE VALUE

Whenever reference is made to Christ's satisfaction of the demands of divine justice, it is also necessary to consider the doctrine of the infinite worth of Jesus Christ. How can one Man suffering on a cross for a few hours make payment for the sins of a nearly countless multitude of sinners and save them from an eternity of suffering in hell? How can the life of that one Man satisfy the justice of an absolutely holy God? The answer is found in the nature of the One who suffered and died. Since the Son of God was the fullness of deity in bodily form (Colossians 2:9), His life was of infinite worth—of infinitely greater worth than all those for whom He died. This is one of the most beautiful truths in all of Scripture.

PROPITIATION IN THE SCRIPTURES

In the following, we will consider some of the most important texts in the Scriptures that refer to Christ's sacrifice as the propitiation for our sins.

1. What do the following texts teach us about Christ as the propitiation for our sins?

    a. *I John 2:2*

    _____

    _____

    _____

    _____

    NOTES: The word "propitiation" comes from the Greek word *hilasmós* (see definition in the introduction to this chapter). The sacrifice of Christ was not limited to the Jews, but also includes a people from every tribe and tongue and people and nation (Revelation 5:9).

    b. *I John 4:10*

    _____

    _____

    _____

    _____

NOTES: The word "propitiation" comes from the Greek word *hilasmós*. God's motivation for sending His Son was His sovereign and unconditional love for His people, which is totally independent of their merit or worth. The ultimate seal or proof of God's love is the propitiating death of His Son for us.

c. *Hebrews 2:17*

_____

_____

_____

_____

NOTES: The phrase "make propitiation" comes from the Greek word *hiláskomai*, the verb form of the noun *hilasmós*. To give help to men, the Son of God had to take upon Himself their nature. It was necessary for a man to die for men (Hebrews 10:4), and only the God-Man could both represent God before man and represent man before God.

2. Like no other text in the Scriptures, Romans 3:23-28 explains the meaning of Christ's death as the propitiation for our sins. Write your comments on each of the following phrases.

a. *Whom God displayed publicly as a propitiation (v.25).*

_____

_____

_____

_____

NOTES: The phrase "displayed publicly" comes from the Greek word *protíthemai*, which means, "to place before or expose to public view." It was God's decree that His Son be publicly crucified in order to clearly reveal His righteousness to all. Here, the word "propitiation" comes from the Greek word *hilastêrion*, which refers to a sacrifice made to expiate, appease, or placate wrath and to obtain favor from an offended party. On the cross, God displayed His Son before the whole world as the propitiation for sin.

b. *In His blood through faith (v.25).*

_____

_____

_____

_____

_____

NOTES: The most natural interpretation of this phrase is that the benefits of Christ's propitiation are received by faith. We are reconciled to God through faith in Christ and His sacrificial (bloody) death on our behalf.

c. *This was to demonstrate His righteousness, because in the forbearance of God He passed over the sins previously committed (v.25).*

_____

_____

_____

_____

_____

NOTES: The great purpose behind God's public display of His Son's death was to demonstrate or prove His righteousness. But why was such a demonstration necessary? The clause cited above reveals to us the answer: "because in the forbearance of God He passed over the sins previously committed." The mercy and forbearance that God has demonstrated toward sinful humanity since the fall of Adam would seem to cast doubt upon His claim to be righteous. Adam and Eve deserved death, but they were granted life; the entire world should have been destroyed during the time of the flood, but sinful Noah and his family were spared; Israel's constant rebellion against the law of God should have resulted in the nation's destruction; David should not have been forgiven his crimes of adultery and murder. How then can God be righteous and yet demonstrate mercy to those who should be condemned? The answer to this question is found in the suffering and death of Christ. God's long forbearance of His people's sin since the fall of Adam was not the result of His apathy or unrighteousness, but was founded upon the future coming of Christ to die for their sin. The mercy, forbearance, and pardon that God lavished upon Old Testament saints who believed in Him were possible only because Christ would come and die for them all! God's past, present, and future mercies are all possible because of the death of Christ. "Although the work of redemption was not actually wrought by Christ until after His incarnation, yet the virtue, efficacy, and benefits thereof were communicated unto the elect in all ages successively from the beginning of the world."[4]

d. *For the demonstration, I say, of His righteousness at the present time, so that He would be just and the justifier of the one who has faith in Jesus (v.26).*

_____

_____

_____

_____

_____

_____

NOTES: In the suffering and death of Jesus Christ on Calvary, every obstacle that would prohibit a righteous God from forgiving His sinful people has been swept away. God demonstrated His righteousness by punishing the sins of His people, satisfying the demands of His justice and appeasing His wrath. He made a way of salvation for His people by standing in their place, bearing their sin, and extinguishing the wrath that was due them in His own body. For this reason, God can justify His people with no contradiction to His own holiness and righteousness.

_____

[4] *Westminster Confession of Faith*, Chapter VIII, Article 6

Chapter 14: Christ Our Liberation

The Scriptures teach not only that fallen man lives under the penalty of the law, but also that he is in bondage to the rule of Satan. Christ redeemed His people from this terrifying reality by dying in their place, thereby both paying the penalty they deserved and disarming Satan of his power.

Before we proceed with our study, it is very important to understand that, although Christ redeemed His people from the power of Satan, the ransom was paid not to Satan but to God. Down through the ages of Christian history, some have wrongly believed that Christ paid a ransom to Satan and thus freed His people from slavery. This clearly contradicts Scripture, diminishes the glory of Christ's redemptive work, and gives to Satan a grossly unbiblical status. The Scriptures teach us that Christ offered Himself as a sacrifice to God in payment for the sins of His people. His death satisfied God's justice and canceled our sin debt, thereby disarming Satan of his power to accuse.

SATAN'S AUTHORITY AND MAN'S BONDAGE

Although God rules over all creation with absolute authority, limited dominion has in a real sense been given to Satan, and through it he rules over this fallen world and its inhabitants.

1. In Luke 4:5-6, Satan makes a declaration about himself and his relationship to this fallen world. What does he declare, and what does it mean?

   _____

   _____

   _____

   _____

   NOTES: At the fall, the world and its inhabitants came under the dominion of Satan. However, we must keep in mind that this dominion is subject to the will of God.

2. Satan's declaration in Luke 4:6 was no idle boast. There is a real sense in which this fallen world lies under his dominion. What does I John 5:19 teach us about this truth?

   a. *The W_____ world lies in the P_____ of the evil one.*

   NOTES: The word "whole" refers not only to mankind collectively but also to every individual outside of Christ. The word "lies" comes from the Greek word *keímai*, which means, "to lie or recline." Mankind in general is not fighting to break free from Satan's rule, but he lives instead in conformity to it.

3. In the Scriptures, a name often communicates something about the person who bears it. What are the names or titles given to Satan in the following Scriptures?

   a. *The R_____ of this W_____ (John 12:31; 14:30; 16:11).* The word "ruler" comes from the Greek word **árchōn**, which may also be translated, "commander" or "chief." This "world" refers to the great mass of humanity that lives in alienation from God and in rebellion against His will.

   b. *The G_____ of this W_____ (II Corinthians 4:4).* There is only one true God (I Corinthians 8:4-6), yet this fallen world follows Satan as though he were its god. Though Satan does not possess the attributes of God, he parades himself as God and desires to be worshiped as God.

   c. *The P_____ of the P_____ of the A_____ (Ephesians 2:2).* Satan is a spirit and is unhindered by the material restraints of man. His power and authority go far beyond any "earthbound" prince. He possesses real power and influence over the spiritually dead (see verse 1).

4. How is fallen man described in the following Scriptures? What is the relationship between fallen man and Satan?

   a. *Fallen man is a child of the D_____ (I John 3:8, 10; John 8:44).* Fallen man is a child of the devil in that he reflects the character and will of the devil. In John 8:44, Jesus declared that the Pharisees were of their father the devil and that they wanted "to do the desires" of their father.

   b. *Fallen man lives under the D_____ of Satan (Acts 26:18).* The word comes from the Greek word **exousía**, which may also be translated, "power" or "authority." Fallen man exists under the authority and power of Satan. In Colossians 1:13, Satan's domain is described as one of spiritual and moral darkness.

   c. *Fallen man walks A_____ to the will of Satan (Ephesians 2:2).* Fallen man is marked by disobedience to God and by walking according to the will of the devil. Fallen men are rightly called "sons of disobedience" in whom the devil is working. The word "working" comes from the Greek word **energéō**, which means, "to be operative; to work effectually or energetically with power."

   d. *Fallen man is B_____ by the devil (II Corinthians 4:4).* Those men who refuse to believe the testimony of God come under a terrifying judgment—they are given over to Satan to be spiritually and morally blinded by his lies and deceptions.

   e. *Fallen man is caught in the S_____ of the devil (II Timothy 2:26).* The word comes from the Greek word **pagís**, which refers to a snare, trap, or noose in which prey would be entangled and captured. It was usually hidden from view and would spring upon its victims and catch them unawares. Fallen men are unknowingly caught in the devil's snare until by the grace of God they come to their senses and escape through the light of the gospel.

f. *Fallen man is H_____ C_____ by the devil (II Timothy 2:26).* The phrase comes from the Greek word ***zōgréō***, which means, "to capture or take alive." By rejecting the benevolent authority of God, fallen man comes under the enslaving authority of Satan. Satan offers fallen man freedom from God's moral law, but this "freedom" always leads to the **bondage** of sin.

g. *Fallen man F_____ Satan (I Timothy 5:15).* The phrase "turned aside" comes from the Greek word ***ektrépō***, which means literally, "to turn or twist out." It was used to describe the act of turning aside to avoid meeting or associating with someone. In a medical context it was used to describe dislocated limbs. Those who turn aside from the will of God demonstrate that they want no part or association with Him. By default, they become "followers" of Satan. Although fallen man may follow Satan ignorantly, he does not follow unwillingly. There is a natural affinity between Satan and fallen man. They are of the same corrupt nature and manifest the same disposition of enmity toward God.

CHRIST'S VICTORY AND OUR REDEMPTION

The Scriptures teach that the penalty of sin is death (Romans 6:23) and that Satan has been granted the power to inflict this penalty upon men (Hebrews 2:14-15). Christ triumphed over Satan through His life, death, and resurrection. By dying in the place of His people, He paid their debt and stripped Satan of his power.

1. In Genesis 3:15, we find an extremely important prophecy regarding the work of the Messiah who would come. According to this prophecy, what would the Christ do to the person and work of the devil? How would He bring about the devil's defeat?

_____

_____

_____

_____

NOTES: This passage is often referred to as the ***protoevangelium*** [Latin: ***proto*** = first + ***evangelium*** = gospel] or "first gospel." The "seed" of woman refers to the Son of God, who, becoming incarnate, would wage war against Satan and conquer him. The Messiah would bruise Satan on the head—He would inflict him with a mortal wound. Satan would bruise the Messiah on the heel—Christ would suffer in His battle with the serpent (Isaiah 53:4-5), but the wound would not ultimately be fatal: the Messiah would rise again! According to Romans 16:20, God's people will share in the Messiah's victory: "The God of peace will soon crush Satan under your feet."

2. What does I John 3:8 teach us about the purpose of Christ's coming?

_____

_____

_____

_____

_____

NOTES: The word "destroy" comes from the Greek word **lúō**, which refers to loosening, undoing, breaking up, or destroying. Christ's coming destroyed the works of the devil, especially with regard to the bondage of His people.

3. What does Colossians 2:15 teach with regard to Christ's triumph over the devil and His work of redemption on behalf of His people?

_____

_____

_____

_____

_____

NOTES: The phrase, "rulers and authorities," is a reference to Satan and the fallen angels. The basis for Satan's power over God's people was their sin, which separated them from God, brought them under the curse, and exposed them to the penalty of death. When Christ interposed and paid the penalty or debt for His people's sin, Satan's power over them was undone. The word "disarmed" comes from the Greek word **apekdúomai**, which means, "to strip off, despoil, or disarm." The phrase "public display" comes from the Greek word **deigmatízō**, which means, "to make an example of or to show as an example." Christ was publicly displayed as our propitiation (Romans 3:25), and His death on Calvary brought about Satan's public defeat. Christ's triumph over the devil and his angels was through the cross, where He bore our sin, suffered in our place, and canceled the certificate of debt against us. The removal of sin brought an end to death and the devil's power to inflict it!

4. What does Hebrews 2:14-15 teach us regarding Christ's triumph over the devil and His work of redemption on behalf of His people?

_____

_____

_____

_____

_____

_____

NOTES: The word "share" comes from the Greek word *koinōnéō*, which means, "to fellowship, take part, or commune together." All men share a common fellowship in flesh and blood and a common communion in its fallen sorrows. The eternal Son of God joined our fellowship of flesh and blood and drank from our communion cup of misery. The devil had power over death in that he could rightly accuse mankind of sin and demand the just penalty of death. Christ paid that penalty and silenced all accusations.

Chapter 15: Christ Our Reconciliation

Part One: The Doctrine of Reconciliation

The one question that most world religions have in common is: "How can a sinful man be reconciled to a just God?" While all other religions point to man's works as a means of reconciliation, the Scriptures point away from man to the person and work of Jesus Christ. Sinful man may be reconciled to God only through Christ's work on Calvary.

WHAT IS RECONCILIATION?

The word "reconcile" comes from the Latin word **reconciliare** [**re** = again, anew + **conciliare** = to assemble, unite, win over]. It means, "to bring together again, to unite anew, to bring into agreement, to make favorable or receptive, to restore friendship or harmony." In the New Testament, "reconcile" and "reconciliation" are translated from the following Greek words.

diallássō: To change or to change the mind; to reconcile; to renew a relationship with another. This word is only used in Matthew 5:24, with regard to being reconciled to an offended brother.

katallássō: To change or exchange, as one might exchange coins for others of equivalent value; to reconcile; to return to favor. In I Corinthians 7:11, it refers to reconciliation between a woman and her husband. In Romans 5:10 (twice) and II Corinthians 5:18-20 (three times), it is used with reference to reconciliation with God.

apokatallássō: A stronger or more intense form of **katallássō**; it refers to reconciling completely. It is used in Ephesians 2:16 and Colossians 1:20 and 22 with reference to God.

katallagê: A noun related to the verb **katallássō**. In secular literature, the word refers to an exchange made in the business of moneychangers, the exchanging of equivalent values, or the adjustment of differences. Figuratively, it refers to reconciliation or restoration to the favor of another. In the New Testament, it refers to the restoration of God's favor to sinners who repent and put their faith in the person and work of Christ (Romans 5:11; 11:15; II Corinthians 5:18-19).

WHO WAS RECONCILED TO WHOM?

Having considered the biblical definitions of the terms "reconcile" and "reconciliation," we are brought to a very important question: "Who was reconciled to whom?" That is, did the cross reconcile man to God (*i.e.* make man favorably disposed to God) or God to man (*i.e.* make God favorably disposed to man)?

This question is important because some erroneously believe that although sinful man is at enmity with God (*i.e.* against God), God is never at enmity with man (*i.e.* against man). However, the Bible teaches that God is also at enmity with the sinner. He is just and holy; therefore, He is angry with the sinner (Psalm 5:5; 7:11; John 3:36), estranged from the sinner (Psalm 5:4; Isaiah 59:2), and disposed to judge the sinner (Psalm 7:11-13; 11:5-6).

Therefore, our answer to the question, "Who was reconciled to whom?" is two-fold. First, **the cross reconciled God to us** in that Christ paid our sin debt, satisfying the justice of God and appeasing His wrath. This removed God's enmity against us and made it possible for Him to justify us through faith in His Son. Second, **we are reconciled to God through the cross** when, through the regenerating and quickening work of the Holy Spirit, we repent of our sin (*i.e.* cease our hostility in thought and deed) and place our faith in Christ.

1. In Romans 5:10-11 is found one of the most important texts in the Scriptures with regard to the doctrine of reconciliation. Read the text until you are familiar with its contents, and then write your thoughts on the following phrases. What do they teach us about biblical reconciliation?

   a. *For if while we were enemies (v.10).*

   _____

   _____

   _____

   _____

   NOTES: The word "enemy" comes from the Greek adjective **echthrós**, which refers to someone who is hostile, hateful, or in bitter opposition to another. In the Gospels, it is used to describe the devil (Matthew 13:39; Luke 10:19); in Romans 8:7 and Colossians 1:21, it is used to describe the "hostile" mind or thoughts of fallen man. It is often held that man is the enemy of God, but God is never the enemy of man. However, this statement is very misleading. Although the enmity or hostility described in verse 10 is mutual, many theologians place the emphasis on God's holy hostility or righteous indignation toward sinful man. Charles Hodge writes, "There is not only a wicked opposition of the sinner to God, but a holy opposition of God to the sinner."[5] Robert L. Reymond writes, "The word 'enemies' does not highlight our unholy hatred of God but rather God's holy hatred of us."[6] Matthew Henry writes, "This enmity is a mutual enmity, God loathing the sinner, and the sinner loathing God."[7]

   b. *We were reconciled to God through the death of His Son (v.10).*

   _____

   _____

---

[5] *Commentary on the Epistle to the Romans*, p.138
[6] *A New Systematic Theology of the Christian Faith*, p.646
[7] *Matthew Henry Commentary*, Vol.6, p.397

NOTES: The Old Testament priests entered into the earthly sanctuary with the blood of animals. Christ offered the sacrifice of Himself on the cross of Calvary and entered into the very presence of God.

b. *Verse 12*

_____

_____

_____

_____

_____

NOTES: Having shed His blood at Calvary, Christ appeared before God in heaven as His people's Representative. This verse does not teach that Christ presented His blood to God in heaven.

c. *Verses 13-14*

_____

_____

_____

_____

_____

_____

NOTES: If the blood of animals offered by sinful priests in an earthly sanctuary provided ceremonial or external cleansing for the unclean, then the blood of Christ is able to do much more! Our good works cannot quiet our nagging conscience, which declares us to be sinners in spite of all our futile attempts to be righteous. The once-and-for-all sacrifice of Christ is able to take away every sin, cleanse the conscience of all guilt, and free us to serve God with peace and joy.

4. One of the most important truths regarding Christ's sacrifice is that it was offered once and for all for every sin of the people of God. In the book of Hebrews, this truth is a recurring theme. Write your thoughts on each of the following texts.

a. *Hebrews 9:25-26*

_____

_____

_____

_____

_____

NOTES: The great superiority of Christ's sacrifice as compared to those of the Old Covenant is that His one sacrifice put an end to His people's sin once and for all.

b. *Hebrews 9:27-28*

_____

_____

_____

_____

NOTES: Christ's sacrifice for sin is so complete that His return for His people will be to bring salvation, without any reference to their sins.

c. *Hebrews 10:12*

_____

_____

_____

NOTES: The contrast is made between the priest, who is "standing daily," (v.11) and Christ, who has "sat down." That Christ has sat down at the right hand of the Father is evidence that His work is complete.

d. *Hebrews 10:14*

NOTES: To be in a right relationship with God, a man must be perfect, entirely separated from sin and separated to God. What is impossible for sinful man has been made possible in Christ. All those who trust in Christ and His sacrifice are given a perfect standing before God, one that is unchanging and eternal. Their sins and lawless deeds He will remember no more (v.17).

Chapter 18: Christ the Lamb

Closely associated with the theme of sacrifice is the Scripture's reference to Christ as the "Lamb of God." The lamb played an important role in the history and worship of Israel. Under the Old Testament sacrificial system, a lamb without spot was offered in the daily morning and evening sacrifices (Exodus 29:38-39). On the Sabbath, the number of offerings was doubled (Numbers 28:9-10). Also, it was a lamb that was slain in the Passover, the religious festival that commemorated God's deliverance of Israel from the land of Egypt and the terrible bonds of slavery.

Although the metaphor of a lamb certainly suggests the gentleness and meekness of Christ's demeanor, this is not its primary significance. In light of the historical background, the picture of Christ as the "Lamb" points primarily to Him as the atoning sacrifice for the sins of His people.

CHRIST THE SACRIFICIAL LAMB

The lamb played an important role in the Old Testament sacrificial system. However, such sacrifices were mere shadows and types that pointed to the one Lamb who would come to take away the sins of the world! That Lamb is Jesus Christ of Nazareth.

1. How does John the Baptist refer to Jesus Christ in John 1:29 and 1:36? What are the truths communicated? Write your thoughts.

_____

_____

_____

_____

_____

NOTES: Being a member of the priestly family, John the Baptist was more than familiar with the themes of the sacrificial lamb and the lamb of the Passover. The fact that John's designation appears twice is very significant (1:29, 36). John the Baptist saw Jesus not as a political deliverer or merely a role model, but as the sacrificial Lamb appointed by God to take away the sins of the world. The phrase "takes away" comes from the Greek word **airō**, which carries the idea of lifting or taking up. With reference to Christ, it means that He took up our sins and bore them away. The verb is in the present tense, indicating a continuous action. The power or efficacy of Christ's death continues to the end of the world. The word "sin" is in the singular, indicating sin as a whole—the totality of every kind and type of sin.

2. In Isaiah 53:6-7 is a description of God's people and the work of the Messiah on their behalf. How does Isaiah's description parallel that of John the Baptist in John 1:29?

_____

_____

_____

_____

_____

NOTES: The word "astray" comes from the Hebrew word **ta`ah**, which means, "to err, go astray, wander about, or stagger." It is sometimes used with reference to intoxication. All men have strayed from God and are as intoxicated men who stagger in their drunkenness. The phrase, "each of us has turned to his own way," proves that all men have followed a way that seems right to them, but its end is the way of death (Proverbs 14:12). To save us, it was necessary that Christ bear our iniquity and be led to the slaughter as our Substitute. Here we see that John the Baptist was not the first prophet to refer to the Messiah as the Lamb who would bear the sin of His people.

3. In I Peter 1:18-20, we find one of the most beautiful texts in all of Scripture regarding the person and work of Christ. In this text, how does Peter refer to Jesus Christ and His work of salvation on behalf of His people? Read the text several times until you are familiar with its contents, and then write your thoughts on the following verses.

a. *You were not redeemed with perishable things like silver or gold from your futile way of life inherited from your forefathers (v.18).*

_____

_____

_____

_____

NOTES: The word "redeemed" comes from the Greek word **lutróō**, which means, "to buy back someone or something from slavery or captivity." In this context, the believer is redeemed from the futile or vain way of life that he has inherited from his forefathers. This can apply to the pagan or Jew. The traditions, religious rituals, and moral codes of Jew and Gentile alike have no power to save.

b. *But with precious blood, as of a lamb unblemished and spotless, the blood of Christ (v.19).*

_____

_____

_____

_____

_____

NOTES: According to Leviticus 22:20-24, an unblemished lamb was required as an offering. According to Peter, Christ is that Lamb. The Scriptures declare, "For the redemption of [a man's] soul is costly, and he should cease trying forever" (Psalm 49:8). No payment that a man could make would be enough to redeem his soul. Only the blood shed by Christ on Calvary was sufficient, because it was of infinite value.

CHRIST THE PASSOVER LAMB

It was a lamb that was slain in the Passover, the religious festival that commemorated God's deliverance of Israel out of the land of Egypt and the terrible bonds of slavery. On the night that God judged the Egyptians, each family in Israel was commanded to take the life of a lamb and to spread its blood upon the doorposts and lintel of their house. When the death angel passed through Egypt in judgment, it would "pass over" the people of God when it saw the blood of the lamb that was slain. It is not difficult to see how the Passover lamb is a type of Christ. Man has broken God's law and is under the sentence of death. Christ stood in the place of His condemned people and died on their behalf. Like the Passover lamb of the Old Testament, His blood was shed to deliver His people from death.

1. In Exodus 12:1-24, we are given the biblical account of Israel's deliverance from Egypt through the death of the Passover lamb. Read the text until you are familiar with its contents, and then answer the following questions.

    a. *How is the Passover lamb described in Exodus 12:5? How does this description apply to Christ as the Lamb of God?*

    (1) The lamb shall be U_____.

    NOTES: This word comes from the Hebrew word **tamiym**, which denotes that which is whole, healthy, unimpaired, or innocent. As a result of sin, man is undone, impaired, and guilty. The physically unblemished lamb was a type or symbol of the sinless Christ, who would offer Himself as a sacrifice for the sin of His people.

b. *According to Exodus 12:21, what was to be done to the Passover lamb? How does this same truth apply to Christ as the Lamb of God?*

_____

_____

_____

_____

NOTES: The word "slay" comes from the Hebrew word **shachat**, which may also be translated, "to slaughter." The slaughtering of the Passover lamb prefigured the death of Christ for the redemption of His people. In Revelation 5:9, the heavenly hosts worship Christ, saying, "Worthy are You to take the book and to break its seals; for You were **slain**, and purchased for God with Your blood men from every tribe and tongue and people and nation" (emphasis added).

c. *According to verse 22, what was to be done with the blood of the Passover lamb? What was each Israelite commanded to do after the blood was applied? How does this same truth apply to Christ as the Lamb of God and the Christian's response and relationship to Him?*

_____

_____

_____

_____

NOTES: First, it was necessary that the Israelites believe God and trust in the means of salvation that He had prescribed. It was through the blood of the Passover lamb that they would be saved from the coming judgment. In the same way, we must believe God's testimony concerning His Son (I John 5:9-12)—that His sacrifice for our sin is the only means of redemption and reconciliation with God. Second, it was necessary that the Israelites remain inside their homes under the protection of the blood; to be caught outside would be certain death. In the same way, the believer has no salvation outside of Christ and His atoning work on Calvary. It is only "in Christ" that all the blessings of a renewed relationship with God come to man. Notice how many times the phrase "in Christ" (or "in Him" or "in the Beloved") is used in Ephesians 1:3-13, where Paul describes the blessings of salvation (vv.3, 4, 6, 7, 9, 10 [twice], 12, 13 [twice]).

buried was a prominent member of the Sanhedrin Council which had sentenced Christ to death. Luke points out that he was "a good and righteous man" and that he had not consented to the death of Christ (Luke 23:50-51). His testimony carries great weight. He had nothing in the world to gain and everything to lose by giving Christ a proper burial. Joseph's great risk was born out of love for Christ.

b. *N_____ accompanied Joseph and assisted him in the preparation of Jesus' dead body for burial (John 19:39).* This man was a Pharisee and a ruler of the Jews (John 3:1). The Pharisees conspired with the Sanhedrin to crucify Jesus. Like Joseph, Nicodemus would have been ostracized by his fellow Pharisees for honoring Jesus. His testimony to the death of Christ and participation in His burial are formidable proofs supporting the reality of these events.

c. *P_____ granted permission for Joseph to take the body of Jesus for burial (John 19:38).* The death of Jesus is confirmed by the fact that Pilate granted permission only after a careful investigation to ensure that Jesus was actually dead (Mark 15:44-45).

d. *The manner in which Jesus' body was prepared for burial is also great proof that He had died. Summarize the account from John 19:38-40. How does it demonstrate that Christ was truly dead and not simply in an unconscious state?*

_____

_____

_____

_____

_____

NOTES: If Christ had been alive, would not Joseph and Nicodemus have discovered it? Everyone who came into contact with the body of Christ was convinced of His death— Roman soldiers (Mark 15:44-45; John 19:32-34), Joseph (Luke 23:50-53), Nicodemus (John 19:39), and the women who witnessed the crucifixion and burial (Luke 23:55-56).

WHERE DID CHRIST GO WHEN HE DIED?

The subject of Christ's whereabouts during the three days between His death and resurrection is often misunderstood. However, a close and careful examination of the Scriptures reveals a unity of thought among all the biblical writers. In the interval between His death and resurrection, Christ's spirit did not remain in the tomb, nor did He descend into hell. In Christ's own words to the repentant thief on the cross, He went to "Paradise," the glorious dwelling place of His Father (Luke 23:43). In the following pages, we will examine the most important texts regarding the matter.

PSALM 16:10

> *For You will not abandon my soul to Sheol; nor will You allow Your Holy One to undergo decay.*

The word "Sheol" is a transliteration of the Hebrew word and can be translated, "underworld," "grave," "pit," or "hell." In the context, the psalmist is simply declaring that God would not allow the Messiah's physical body to undergo physical corruption, but would raise Him from the dead. This is the interpretation of Peter (Acts 2:27-31) and of Paul (Acts 13:34-35).

In Acts 2:27, Peter quotes this text in defense of Christ's resurrection: "You will not abandon my soul to Hades." The word *hádēs* is the Greek translation of *sheol* and refers to the same. The simple meaning of the texts is that the Father would not allow the body of Jesus to decompose in the bonds of death, but would raise Him from the dead. Charles Hodge writes, "In Scriptural language, therefore, to descend into Hades means nothing more than to descend to the grave, to pass from the visible into the invisible world, as happens to all men when they die and are buried."[8]

ROMANS 10:7

> *"Who will descend into the abyss?" (that is, to bring Christ up from the dead).*

Based on Paul's own interpretation ("up from the dead"), it seems best to interpret the word "abyss" as a reference to the realm of the dead and not as an assertion that Christ went to hell. Matthew Henry writes, "This plainly shows that Christ's descent into the deep, or into *ábussos*, was no more than his going into the state of the dead."[9]

EPHESIANS 4:9

> *Now [the] expression, "He ascended," what does it mean except that He also had descended into the lower parts of the earth?*

The context suggests that Paul is writing about the incarnation of Christ and not some descent into hell. The Christ who went up to heaven (ascension) is the same who came down to earth from heaven (incarnation). In Isaiah 44:23, we read: "Shout for joy, O heavens, for the Lord has done it! Shout joyfully, you lower parts of the earth; break forth into a shout of joy, you mountains, O forest, and every tree in it; for the Lord has redeemed Jacob and in Israel He shows forth His glory." Here again, the phrase, "lower parts of the earth," simply refers to the earth in contrast to the heavens.

I PETER 3:18-20

> *For Christ also died for sins once for all, the just for the unjust, so that He might bring us to God, having been put to death in the flesh, but made alive in the spirit; in which also He went and made proclamations*

---

[8] *Systematic Theology*, Vol.2, p.617
[9] *Matthew Henry Commentary*, Vol.6, p.439

to the spirits now in prison, who once were disobedient, when the patience of God kept waiting in the days of Noah, during the construction of the ark, in which a few, that is, eight persons, were brought safely through the water.

Some interpret this text as teaching that Christ descended into hell when He died, so that He might proclaim His victory to those who dwelled there. The more consistent interpretation is that the Holy Spirit, who raised Christ from the dead, was the very instrument through whom Christ spoke to Noah's generation. Christ spoke to them through the Holy Spirit, by means of the preaching of Noah. They did not believe the words of Christ preached by Noah; therefore, they died in their sins and have remained in prison (*i.e.* hell) until now.

I Peter 4:6

For the gospel has for this purpose been preached even to those who are dead, that though they are judged in the flesh as men, they may live in the spirit according to the will of God.

There is no reason to interpret this text as pointing to a descent by Christ into hell in order to preach the gospel to those who dwell there. The Scriptures clearly teach that "it is appointed for men to die once and after this comes judgment" (Hebrews 9:27). The text should be interpreted as a simple reference to the gospel that had been preached to certain individuals who, at the time of Peter's writing, had already died.

Luke 23:43

And He [Jesus] said to him [the thief], "Truly I say to you, today you shall be with Me in Paradise."

If Christ did not go to hell, where did He go? To answer this question, it is best to take Christ at His own words. Jesus told the dying thief, "Truly I say to you, today you shall be with Me in Paradise." At Christ's death, His spirit passed immediately into the presence of God. At the resurrection, His body and spirit were once again united. It is significant that the word "Paradise" is used only two other times in the New Testament, and both times it refers clearly to heaven (II Corinthians 12:4; Revelation 2:7).

Luke 23:46

And Jesus, crying out with a loud voice, said, "Father, into your hands I commit My spirit." Having said this, He breathed His last.

In this brief but powerful declaration, we find further evidence that Christ went to be with the Father at the moment of His death. It is a declaration of strong confidence, not unlike "Today, you shall be with Me in paradise." Matthew Henry writes, "[Christ] commends His spirit into His Father's hand, to be received into paradise, and returned the third day."[10]

---

[10] *Matthew Henry Commentary*, Vol.5, p.830

JOHN 20:17

> *Jesus said to her [Mary], "Stop clinging to Me, for I have not yet ascended to the Father; but go to My brethren and say to them, 'I ascend to My Father and your Father, and My God and your God.'"*

It is sometimes argued that Christ could not have ascended to heaven during His three days in the tomb based upon His own words to Mary Magdalene in this passage. However, upon closer consideration, it is clear that there is no contradiction between Christ's statement to the thief (Luke 23:43) and His words to Mary Magdalene (John 20:17). After three days, Christ reunited with His physical body and was raised from the dead. Mary misunderstood the plan of God and was unaware that Christ would ascend again (this time, bodily) to the right hand of the Father as His people's Intercessor. She expected Him to remain on earth and reign as an earthly Messiah. In His interaction with Mary, Christ is not denying that His **spirit** had ascended to the Father following His death on the cross, but is saying that He had yet to ascend **bodily**. Though Mary did not yet realize it, this bodily ascension was absolutely necessary in the work of redemption.

Chapter 21: Christ Has Risen

The following statement is often used to summarize the fullness of the gospel message: "Christ died for our sins." This is a grave error! According to I Corinthians 15:1-4, the gospel of Jesus Christ is not only that He died for the sins of God's people, but also that He rose from the dead on the third day. The resurrection of Christ stands beside His death as one of the two great columns of Christianity. Without the resurrection, the death of Christ would not be good news!

The greatest declaration of hope that has ever been spoken by mortal or angelic tongue is, "Christ has risen!" His resurrection was the great proof of His deity, the vindication of His person, and the guarantee that God had accepted His death as payment for the sins of His people. There are few doctrines more important, and none more attacked by the unbelieving world, than the resurrection of Jesus Christ. The credibility of Christianity and the salvation of those who believe hang upon this one doctrine.

A HISTORICAL EVENT

Webster's Dictionary defines "historicity" as "the quality of being historic, especially as distinct from the mythological or legendary." The account of the advent of the Son of God recorded in the four Gospels (Matthew, Mark, Luke, and John) differs greatly from mythology in that it was an event that actually occurred in the context of human history. The Son of God really came into our world at a specific time and in a specific place. He was a real, historical person, and the account of His life was recorded in writing by those who both knew Him and witnessed His life and teaching. To them, the resurrection of Jesus Christ was neither a myth nor a spiritualized event; it was a historical reality. To treat the resurrection as something other than real history is to deny the testimony of Scripture.

1. In Luke 1:1-4, we find powerful evidence that the writers of the Gospels were fully convinced that they were relating historical fact based upon either their own personal witness or the carefully investigated testimony of others. How does this introduction to Luke's Gospel demonstrate that he believed that he was recording real history?

_____

_____

_____

_____

_____

NOTES: The word "compile" (v.1) comes from the Greek word *anatássomai*, which means, "to put together in order or to arrange." Luke had taken it upon himself to write an orderly and historically correct account of the incarnation of the Son of God and His works. The phrase "handed down" (v.2) comes from the Greek word *paradídōmi*, which means, "to deliver something to another to keep or use; to commit or commend something to someone." The apostles who were with Christ "from the beginning" had been faithful to "hand down" the truth about His person and works. The word "eyewitnesses" (v.2) comes from the Greek word *autóptēs*, which refers to one who sees with his own eyes. The medical term "autopsy," which refers to a detailed examination, is derived from this word. The "eyewitnesses" and "servants of the word" are probably references to the apostles. The word "investigated" (v.3) comes from the Greek word *parakolouthéō*, which means, "to follow after" or "to attend one wherever he goes." Metaphorically, it means to track down a matter or to examine it thoroughly. Luke had carefully followed after the truth and recorded it in his Gospel. The phrase "everything carefully" (v.3) denotes that Luke's investigation was both exhaustive and diligent. He had examined all the available data. His goal was to report historical truth without embellishments. The phrase, "in consecutive order," (v.3) comes from the Greek word *kathexês*, which denotes succession and order. It does not necessarily refer to chronological order, but to a logical and systematic coordination of the facts. The word "exact" (v.4) comes from the Greek word *asphália*, which denotes firmness, stability, or certainty. Luke wrote so that Theophilus might have full certainty about the things he had been taught.

2. In Luke's writing of the book of Acts, he gives an introduction similar to that found in his Gospel. How does Acts 1:3 demonstrate that Luke saw himself as recording historical fact when he wrote about the resurrection?

_____

_____

_____

_____

_____

NOTES: The phrase "convincing proofs" comes from the Greek work *tekmêrion*, which may be translated, "solid evidence" or "plain indications." There are thirteen post-resurrection appearances of Christ recorded in the New Testament. If Christ had made a single brief appearance to one individual, there would be room for reasonable doubt; but several appearances to many people over a period of forty days strengthens the testimony of the early disciples. The phrase, "speaking of the things concerning the kingdom of God," is extremely important. Christ did not simply appear and disappear; rather, He tarried with His disciples and taught them as He had before His death. The apostles and early disciples did not base their testimony upon phantom-like appearances, but upon real, personal fellowship with the risen Christ (see also Luke 24:27).

3. In Acts 10:38-42 is recorded the Apostle Peter's sermon to those who would become the first Gentile converts. Read the account, and follow the apostle's reasoning in verses 40-42 for the historicity of Christ's resurrection.

   a. *God R_____ Him up on the T_____ day (v.40)*. This was God's validation of the person and work of Jesus of Nazareth (Romans 1:4). All of Christianity stands and falls on this truth. It is for this reason that the resurrection is so frequently proclaimed in the New Testament.

   b. *And granted that He become V_____ (v.40)*. Christ's appearances were demonstrations of God's graciousness to His people.

   c. *Not to all the people, but to W_____ who were C_____ beforehand by God (v.41)*. Like all the miracles of His earthly ministry, Christ's post-resurrection appearances were under God's sovereign direction and had a specific purpose—the building up of His church. Christ did not appear to the unbelieving masses in order to vindicate Himself. This will, however, happen at His second coming.

   d. *That is, to us who A_____ and D_____ with Him after He arose from the dead (v.41)*. Christ did not merely appear as an ethereal phantom or fleeting vision; He fellowshipped with His people and gave them certain proofs of His bodily resurrection (John 20:26-27; 21:9-14).

   e. *And He ordered us...solemnly to T_____ (v.42)*. This phrase comes from the Greek word **diamartúromai**, which denotes testifying with great earnestness, seriousness, and even gravity.

   f. *That this is the One who has been A_____ by God as J_____ of the living and the dead (v.42)*. The resurrection is proof that Christ is Savior (Acts 4:12), Lord (Acts 2:36), and Judge (Acts 17:31).

   g. *How does this passage demonstrate that Peter viewed Christ's resurrection as a real event in history?*

   _____

   _____

   _____

   _____

4. In I Corinthians 15:3-9 is found still another account of the amount of evidence supporting the validity of the resurrection. Fill in the blanks with those whom the Apostle Paul lists as having seen the risen Christ.

   a. *To C_____ (v.5)*. This is a reference to Peter (John 1:42). This appearance, recorded in Luke 24:34, occurred the day of Christ's resurrection.

b. *To the T_____ (v.5).* Although Judas is no longer among the apostles and their number has been reduced to eleven, they are still referred to as "the twelve." This post-resurrection appearance is one of several by Jesus to His disciples (see verse 7); it occurred on the evening of the resurrection and is recorded in Luke 24:36-43 and John 20:19-23.

c. *To more than F_____ H_____ brethren at one time (v.6).* This is possibly a reference to Acts 1:6-11. The fact that Christ appeared to five hundred witnesses collectively (*i.e.* at the same time and place) makes it highly unlikely that it was a case of mistaken identity or hallucination. According to the Old Testament Law, "on the evidence of two or three witnesses a matter shall be confirmed" (Deuteronomy 19:15). The fact that most of the five hundred were still alive at the time of Paul's writing and could be called upon to testify gives further support to Paul's argument.

d. *To J_____ (v.7).* This is a reference to the half brother of Jesus (Matthew 13:55). He did not believe the messianic claims of Jesus (John 7:5) until after the resurrection, when he joined the apostles (Acts 1:14) and became one of the most prominent leaders among the early Christians (Acts 15:13ff).

e. *To one U_____ born (v.8).* This phrase comes from the Greek word **éktrōma**, which refers to a miscarriage or an abortive birth. Paul was not one of the original twelve apostles who walked with Christ during His earthly ministry, but was converted later, when he was confronted by Christ while on his way to Damascus (Acts 9:3-6, 17).

f. *In your own words, explain how this text demonstrates that Paul regarded the resurrection as a real, historical event.*

_____

_____

_____

_____

NOTES: By listing in chronological order the post-resurrection appearances of Christ, the Apostle Paul demonstrated that he viewed Christ's resurrection as a real event in history—one that was validated by eyewitness testimony.

THE BIBLICAL ACCOUNT

Before we consider Christ's resurrection any further, it will be helpful to consider a thorough summary of the historical events as they are described to us in the Scriptures.

It is early morning on the third day after Jesus' death. The women make their way timidly to the garden where the body of Christ has been entombed. Theirs is an errand not of hope but of pity. Their only desire is to honor the body of their beloved Jesus with a proper burial.

Their conversation is limited to what would become a minor technicality: "Who will roll away the stone?" (Mark 16:2-4). Resurrection is the farthest thing from their minds. However, pity turns to fear, fear to hope unquenchable, and hope to joy unspeakable and full of glory! They are greeted with a displaced stone, an opened door, an empty tomb, and an angelic proclamation of good news: "Why do you seek the living One among the dead? He is not here, but He has risen" (Luke 24:5-8).

The women quickly depart from the tomb "with fear and great joy" (Matthew 28:8). They run to bring His disciples the word, but their testimony appears as idle talk and nonsense to the very ones who should have believed them (Luke 24:11). Then, hoping against hope, Peter and John run to the empty tomb. After a brief and perplexing investigation, they return to the others without a sure word: "For as yet they did not understand the Scriptures, that He must rise again from the dead" (John 20:9).

In their quick departure, they leave behind the weeping Mary Magdalene, who becomes the first to see the risen Lord. She is then commissioned by Him to return once more to the unbelieving disciples with still another confirmation of His resurrection (John 20:11-18). This is followed by a second appearance, to the women returning from the tomb (Matthew 28:9-10), and then a third, to Cleopas and another disciple on the road to Emmaus (Luke 24:13-32). At last, He appears to Peter alone (Luke 24:34); then twice to the eleven apostles—first without Thomas (John 20:19-25) and then with him (John 20:26-29)—and again to seven of His disciples by the Sea of Galilee (John 21:1-14). He even appears to His unbelieving half brother James (I Corinthians 15:7), whose life is so altered by the encounter that he becomes part of the apostolic band (Acts 1:14) and a pillar in the church of Jerusalem (Acts 15:13ff). Finally, He appears "to one untimely born" (I Corinthians 15:8), to Saul (later Paul) of Tarsus on the road to Damascus (Acts 9:3-19). It is almost superfluous to write about this encounter or its effect. The very man who had pledged himself to the destruction of Christianity becomes its most ardent propagator and defender (Acts 9:1-2; I Corinthians 15:10).

In the end, we have the sure word of Scripture that before His ascension our Lord appeared to a great number of witnesses, both to individuals and "to more than five hundred brethren at one time" (I Corinthians 15:6).

Chapter 22: The Foundation of Our Faith in the Resurrection

THE REALITY OF THE RESURRECTION

This chapter is the briefest in this study, but it is one of the most important with regard to the believer's faith in Christ and His resurrection.

The enemies of Christianity are right in focusing their attacks on the historical resurrection of Christ, because, as Paul points out in I Corinthians 15, the entirety of our faith depends upon it! If Christ has not been raised, then our faith is utterly worthless (vv.14, 17): those of us who believe are still in our sins, and those who have died have perished forever (vv.17-18). Furthermore, it would logically follow that we who preach the resurrection are false witnesses of God, because we testify that He has raised Christ when He has not (v.15). Finally, if Christ has not been raised, then our lives are a pathetic waste: we suffer hardship for no reason and are hated for the sake of a false prophet who has no power to save. As the Apostle Paul writes: "If we have hoped in Christ in this life only, we are of all men most to be pitied" (v.19).

By our own admission, the resurrection is everything to the Christian faith. If Christ has not been raised, our religion is false. Therefore, we would do well to ask ourselves a very important question: "How do we know that Christ truly has been raised?" In these next two chapters, we will break away from the workbook format so that we might consider two very important but fundamentally different mediums through which the reality of the resurrection is made known to us—it is **revealed** to us through the illuminating and regenerating work of the Holy Spirit, and it is **confirmed** to us by the historical evidence that surrounds the event itself. The former is absolutely essential. The latter is a strong confirmation of the Christian faith and an effective tool for dialogue with the unbelieving world.

THE WORK OF THE HOLY SPIRIT

The Protestant Church often attempts to validate its faith in the resurrection by pointing to the empty tomb, the inability of Christ's enemies to present a cadaver, the transformation of the disciples, and many other historical and legal proofs. However, although these do demonstrate that the Christian faith is not illogical or counterhistorical, they should not be seen as the **basis** or **foundation** of the Christian's faith. This will be demonstrated by the following facts.

First, the apostles did not use this form of argumentation in their preaching. They did not strive to prove the resurrection, but to proclaim it (Acts 4:2, 33; 17:18; 24:21). Their confidence did not rest in their powerful arguments, but in the power of the gospel to save! Consider what the Apostle Paul penned in his first epistle to the church in Corinth:

> *For the word of the cross is foolishness to those who are perishing, but to us who are being saved it is the power of God… For indeed Jews ask for signs and Greeks search for wisdom; but we preach Christ crucified,*

*to Jews a stumbling block and to Gentiles foolishness, but to those
who are the called, both Jews and Greeks, Christ the power of God
and the wisdom of God. (1:18, 22-24)*

*And when I came to you, brethren, I did not come with superiority of
speech or of wisdom, proclaiming to you the testimony of God. For
I determined to know nothing among you except Jesus Christ, and
Him crucified. I was with you in weakness and in fear and in much
trembling, and my message and my preaching were not in persuasive
words of wisdom, but in demonstration of the Spirit and of power, so
that your faith would not rest on the wisdom of men, but on the power
of God. (2:1-5)*

Second, the overwhelming majority of those who have converted to Christianity throughout
church history, including its greatest intellectuals, were not brought to faith by studying the historical and legal evidence regarding the resurrection, but by sitting under the proclamation of
the gospel.

Third, if our faith in the resurrection is founded upon its historical and legal evidence, how
can we explain the faith of countless believers who lived and died for their faith without the
slightest knowledge of such evidence? How do we explain the tribal Christian who can barely
read and is unable to offer one historical argument for the resurrection, yet will endure the
most despicable persecutions and even martyrdom rather than deny the faith that he is unable
to logically defend? In light of these truths, we must conclude that although the historical and
legal evidence for the resurrection is **helpful** in many ways, it is **not the foundation** of our faith
in the resurrection.

What then is the foundation of the believer's faith in the resurrection? How does he know
that Christ has been raised? The answer from the Scriptures is clear. We owe our knowledge
and unwavering faith in the resurrection to the regenerating and illuminating work of the Holy
Spirit! Our conviction regarding the reality of the resurrection of Jesus Christ and the validity of
the Christian faith is supernaturally imparted to us at the moment of the new birth (John 3:3).
We know that Christ has risen from the dead because the Holy Spirit has illumined our minds
to the truth of the Scriptures as they bear witness to Christ (John 5:39; I John 5:6-10). In short,
we believe because the Spirit regenerates our hearts, imparting faith and new affections for the
Christ who has been revealed to us. The Apostle Paul describes this miraculous work of the Spirit
in II Corinthians 4:6:

*For God, who said, "Light shall shine out of darkness," is the One who
has shone in our hearts to give the Light of the knowledge of the glory
of God in the face of Christ.*

Those who have been born again can no more deny the resurrection of Jesus Christ than
they can deny their own existence. By God's sovereign decree and the witness of the Holy
Spirit, it has become an incontestable reality to them (Matthew 11:25). As the persecutors
of the Christian faith have learned, "For those infected with the religion of Jesus, there is no
cure."[11]

---

[11] This is said to be the testimony of Soviet soldiers who sought to turn Christians from their faith in the living Christ.

The truths we have learned serve as both a warning and a directive. Although apologetics[12] has its place, the Kingdom of Heaven advances primarily through the proclamation of the gospel. Men will come to faith not through our eloquence or logical arguments, but through our faithful proclamation of the life, death, and resurrection of Jesus Christ. We must never forget that our mission is a fool's errand and that our labor is a waste of time and effort unless the Spirit of God is working to illuminate the minds and regenerate the hearts of our hearers. For this reason, we must refuse to lean upon the broken staff of human wisdom (Isaiah 36:6); we must cling instead to the truth that the gospel alone is the power of God unto salvation for all who believe (Romans 1:16).

---

[12] Apologetics is a discipline often used to defend the Christian faith; its proponents employ logical or reasoned arguments in order to demonstrate errors in the counterarguments of Christianity's opponents.

Chapter 23: Evidence for the Resurrection of Christ

An individual's faith in Christ is not dependent upon his or her ability to recite the historical or legal evidence regarding Christ's resurrection. Nor does it stand or fall according to the believer's ability to defend its validity through the use of apologetics or classical logic. Nevertheless, it is important to recognize and proclaim that the Christian faith is not contrary to history or to the highest and most pristine use of reason. True Christianity finds no virtue in seeking to transform myth into a useful narrative in order to promote some moral good in the world. Rather, the Christian faith and belief in the resurrection of Jesus Christ are grounded in actual events of history that can be abundantly substantiated through the same types and kinds of proofs that are used by the "secular historian."

Those who reject the claims of Christianity as unhistorical or mythological do so because of biased presuppositions that will not allow the evidence to speak for itself; and they do so, says Robert Reymond, on "highly questionable critical and philosophical grounds with which they are simply more comfortable psychologically and religiously."[13] Their logic is perilous: they have decided beforehand that the resurrection is an impossibility; therefore, every piece of evidence in favor of the legitimacy of this event must be fallacious, and every claim to its credibility must be the deduction of a fool or the invention of a charlatan.

The adverseness of sinful men toward the gospel is one more reason to assert that apart from the grace of God and the regenerating work of the Holy Spirit, no man will accept the claims of Christ. Man will ignore the claims he can, distort the claims he cannot ignore, and resist the claims he cannot distort. In other words, he will expend more energy denying the truth than he would have expended by simply submitting to it.

Although it is beyond the scope of this workbook to consider *all* of the evidence that substantiates Christ's resurrection, we will explore in this chapter some of the legal and logical proofs that are most beneficial to both the believer's faith and the seeker's inquiries.

A PREDICTED EVENT

The death and the resurrection of Jesus Christ were not unpredicted events that caught Him unawares; each was clearly prophesied as a necessary fulfillment of the will of God. This is evident in Jesus' words in Luke 24:25-26, which He spoke to His doubting disciples after His resurrection:

> *O foolish men and slow of heart to believe in all that the prophets have spoken! Was it not necessary for the Christ to suffer these things and to enter into His glory?*

The resurrection of the Messiah was clearly revealed in Old Testament prophecies written hundreds of years before His coming. David predicted that God would not abandon the Messiah to the grave, nor allow His body to undergo decay (Psalm 16:8-11). The prophet Isaiah looked ahead

---

[13] *A New Systematic Theology of the Christian Faith*, p.581.

and saw that God would greatly reward the Messiah after He had suffered the sins of His people unto death (Isaiah 53:12). Christ Himself predicted His death and resurrection long before His crucifixion. When the unbelieving Jews asked Him for a sign or proof of His authority to cleanse the temple, He declared: "Destroy this temple, and in three days I will raise it up" (John 2:19). When the scribes and Pharisees asked Him for further proof of His messianic claims, His rebuke was accompanied by the promise of His future resurrection:

> An evil and adulterous generation craves for a sign; and yet no sign will be given to it but the sign of Jonah the prophet; for just as Jonah was three days and three nights in the belly of the sea monster, so will the Son of Man be three days and three nights in the heart of the earth. (Matthew 12:39-40)

These prophecies show that Christ's disciples did not invent the resurrection as a desperate attempt to keep the messianic dream alive. Christ declared it so clearly and so often (Matthew 16:21) that even His enemies knew of His predictions that He would rise again:

> Now on the next day, the day after the preparation, the chief priests and the Pharisees gathered together with Pilate, and said, "Sir, we remember that when He was still alive that deceiver said, 'After three days I am to rise again.'" (Matthew 27:62-63)

THE EMPTY TOMB

With all the attention given to the body of Jesus after His death, not only by His disciples but also by His enemies, an empty tomb and an undiscovered cadaver is strong evidence of a resurrection. From the very first day, all that was needed to destroy Christianity was the presentation of the dead body of the Man Jesus. The Jewish leaders who called for His death and the Roman authorities who crucified Him knew the exact location of the tomb and had ample opportunity to exhume the body. If the tomb was not empty, then with one bold move they could have proven to the world that the Easter message was a hoax and that the apostles were devious perpetrators of a myth. Christianity would have died in its very infancy. Why was the body never produced?

Skeptics have invented three theories in response to this question. All are equally absurd. The first, often called the "Swoon Theory," is that Jesus did not die upon the Roman cross; rather, He only lost consciousness and was improperly diagnosed. Later, when placed in the cool tomb, He regained consciousness and escaped. The arguments against such a theory are founded upon the nature of the crucifixion itself—He was pierced through His side with a Roman spear and declared dead after a thorough examination by experts (John 19:31-34). Even if He had somehow survived the ordeal, He would have hardly been in any condition to move the heavy stone that blocked the tomb's entrance. Furthermore, it seems highly unlikely at best that such a personality would have been able to escape into some unknown region of Palestine and live out the rest of His life in anonymity.

The second theory is that the disciples stole the body and reburied it in some unknown location. The arguments against such a theory come from two sources. The first is the fierce reputation of the Roman guard, whose character and efficiency is legendary. The second is the New Testament's account of the disciples' fear during and after Christ's death. The Scriptures tell us that immediately after the death of Christ, the chief priests and Pharisees asked Pilate to secure the tomb with a trained Roman guard in order to prevent the disciples from stealing His body and perpetuating the myth that Christ had resurrected (Matthew 27:64). It is highly improbable that a handful of frightened disciples could overpower an entire Roman guard in order to steal the body of Jesus. The disciples had already shown their lack of courage by deserting Christ during the crucifixion (Mark 14:27; Matthew 26:56), and the leader among them, Simon Peter, could not even stand up to a servant girl when she identified him as one of Christ's followers (Luke 22:55-62). It is also equally improbable that an entire Roman guard would fall asleep on duty, as the chief priests suggested (Matthew 28:11-15). In fact, it takes more faith to believe this theory than it does to accept the resurrection!

The third theory is that the disciples simply went to the wrong tomb. This also is highly unlikely in light of the fact that the tomb belonged to Joseph of Arimathea, a member of the Sanhedrin council (Matthew 27:57-61; Mark 15:42-47; Luke 23:50-56). He and Nicodemus, a man of the Pharisees and a ruler of the Jews (John 3:1), were the very men who prepared the body of Jesus for burial and placed Him in the tomb (John 19:38-42). Furthermore, the Scriptures tell us that the women who had followed Jesus from Galilee also knew the exact location of the tomb (Matthew 27:61, Mark 15:47; Luke 23:55). If the disciples had gone to the wrong tomb, it is certain that friend and foe alike would have corrected their mistake by bringing them to the correct tomb, unwrapping the body, and showing them the physical remains of Jesus.[14] This theory joins the others in its absurdity.

CREDIBLE WITNESSES

For an event to be confirmed as historical or real, three things are required: (1) there must be eyewitnesses; (2) these eyewitnesses must be sufficient in number; and (3) they must demonstrate integrity or trustworthiness.[15] It is significant that all of these requirements are met in the Scriptures' testimony regarding the resurrection of Jesus Christ.

First, the Scriptures' testimony is founded upon eyewitness accounts of Christ's ministry, resurrection, and ascension. Every author of the New Testament stands with the Apostle Peter when he declared in II Peter 1:16:

> For we did not follow cleverly devised tales when we made known to
> you the power and coming of our Lord Jesus Christ, but we were eye-
> witnesses of His majesty.

The importance of first-hand or eyewitness testimony is clearly recognized by the writers of the New Testament. To be joined to the Eleven, Matthias had to be an eyewitness of Christ's life and ministry—beginning with the baptism of John, continuing through the resurrection, and lasting even to the day that Christ ascended into heaven (Acts 1:21-26). In writing his Gospel, Luke took great pains to emphasize that he was compiling "an account of things" that "were handed down…by those who from the beginning were eyewitnesses" (Luke 1:1-4). The Apostle John begins his first epistle (vv.1-4) by powerfully and eloquently affirming the personal relationship with Christ the Son with which all the apostles were privileged—a relationship that also formed the basis for both their doctrine and proclamation to others:

---

[14] Robert Reymond, *A New Systematic Theology of the Christian Faith*, p.566.
[15] Henry Thiessen, *Lectures in Systematic Theology*, p.246.

What was from the beginning, what we have heard, what we have seen with our eyes, what we have looked at and touched with our hands, concerning the Word of Life—and the life was manifested, and we have seen and testify and proclaim to you the eternal life, which was with the Father and was manifested to us—what we have seen and heard we proclaim to you also, so that you too may have fellowship with us; and indeed our fellowship is with the Father, and with His Son Jesus Christ. These things we write, so that our joy may be made complete.

It should be clear to any unbiased examiner that the apostles both possessed a personal, first-hand knowledge of Christ's life, death, and resurrection and recognized the importance of affirming the nature of their knowledge as such. They wanted the world to know that they had not been misled by hearsay, but had touched the hands, feet, and side of the resurrected Christ (Luke 24:39; John 20:27). They had fellowshipped with Him (Luke 24:13-32, 36-43; John 21:12-14), and they had been instructed by Him (Luke 24:44-49). Finally, they had worshiped Him as He passed from their view into heaven (Luke 24:50-53).

Second, for an event to be confirmed as historical or real, there must be a sufficient number of eyewitnesses. To put it plainly, the more eyewitnesses there are, the more credible the event is. This same principle is found both in the Law of the Old Testament and in the New Testament commands to the church—an event is to be confirmed only on the testimony of at least two or three witnesses (Deuteronomy 17:6; 19:15; Matthew 18:16).

In the case of Christ's resurrection, this requirement has also been satisfied. The Scriptures report that there were hundreds of credible witnesses who encountered the risen Christ in a variety of situations and circumstances. On Resurrection Sunday, He appeared to Mary Magdalene in the garden (John 20:11-18), then again to the small group of women who were returning from the tomb (Matthew 28:9-10). On the same day, He joined Cleopas and another disciple as they walked together on the road to Emmaus (Mark 16:12-13; Luke 24:13-32). Before the day had passed, He revealed Himself also to Peter (Luke 24:34) and then to ten disciples in the upper room (Luke 24:36-43; John 20:19-25). On the following Sunday, He appeared to all eleven apostles and had His famous discourse with doubting Thomas (Mark 16:14; John 20:26-29; I Corinthians 15:5). After that, He appeared to more than five hundred witnesses at one time (I Corinthians 15:6) and to His half brother James (I Corinthians 15:7). At some undisclosed time, He came again to Peter, John, and five other disciples as they were fishing on the Sea of Tiberias (John 21:1-14). Finally, He ascended into heaven in the presence of His disciples on the Mount of Olives (Luke 24:50-53; Acts 1:9-11).

In light of the testimony of Scripture, it is impossible to discredit the account of Christ's resurrection based upon some false notion that it lacked a sufficient number of eyewitnesses. To this truth, the great English preacher Charles Spurgeon eloquently testifies:

Does it not strike you that very many events of the greatest importance recorded in history, and commonly believed, could not in the nature of things have been witnessed by one-tenth as many as the resurrection of Christ? The signing of famous treaties affecting nations, the births of princes, the remarks of cabinet ministers, the projects of conspirators, and the deeds of assassins—any and all of these have been made turning points in history and are never questioned as facts, and yet but few could have been present to witness them... If this fact [*i.e.* the resurrection] is to be denied, there is an end to all witness, and we have said deliberately what David said in haste: "All men are liars"; and from this day forth every man must become so skeptical of his neighbor, that he will never believe anything which he has not himself seen; the next step will be to doubt the evidence of his own senses; to what further follies men may then rush, I will not venture to predict.[16]

Finally, for an event to be confirmed as historical or real, the eyewitnesses must demonstrate their integrity. In other words, they must prove themselves trustworthy. It is no secret that throughout the history of Christianity, countless skeptics have done their best to discredit the New Testament witnesses; however, they have never been able to disprove their sincerity or disqualify them on ethical or moral grounds. For this reason, the skeptics have been forced to focus their attacks on the possibility of self-delusion and mass hysteria.

It has been argued that the disciples and many of the first-century Jews were predisposed to believe in the resurrection; therefore, they simply saw what they wanted to see. Proponents of this view use the following line of reasoning. First, the Jewish nation struggled under the unbearable oppression of the Roman Empire. Because of this, the Jews of Jesus' day were longing for the coming of the Messiah and would have been easily deceived. Many among the Jews had already followed several false messiahs who had arisen among the people (Acts 5:36-37), proving they were willing to believe almost anything. Second, Jesus made many predictions regarding His future resurrection. When combined with the disciples' great love for their beloved teacher, such prophecies would have been perfect soil for the sprouting of self-delusion and mass hysteria.

Standing against these popular theories are several facts. **First**, the vast majority of the Jewish nation rejected Jesus of Nazareth as the Messiah. His earthly ministry and death were a stumbling block to them (I Corinthians 1:23). Adding the resurrection to the already scandalous message of the cross would not have made Jesus' claims to be the Messiah any more compelling to the Jew. Furthermore, this theory does not take into account the fact that within a few decades the vast majority of believers were Gentiles who had no predisposition to believe anything about the gospel. As Lewis and Demarest write:

> The event occurred in sharp antithesis to what they [*i.e.* the Jews] had expected theologically, and it was in genuine conflict with the framework of the secular world view at the time. To the Jew it was a stumbling block and to the Greek nonsense because the evidence required a Copernican revolution in their theology and cosmology.[17]

Second, the Jews and Gentiles were not the only ones who were not predisposed to believe in the resurrection; the same may also be said without reservation about the disciples. Mary Magdalene was the first to see Christ after the resurrection; however, when she first encountered the empty tomb, she believed that someone had stolen the Lord's body and moved it to an unknown location (John 20:2, 13, 15). Even after reports of Christ's resurrection began to emerge, the disciples still did not believe. Luke records that the news of Christ's resurrection "appeared to them as nonsense" (Luke 24:10-11), and Mark writes that they "refused to believe it" (Mark 16:11). In their first

[16] *The Metropolitan Tabernacle Pulpit*, Vol.8, pp.218-219.

[17] *Integrative Theology*, Vol.2, p.466. Nicolaus Copernicus (1473-1543) was the first to suggest a heliocentric cosmology—a model of the solar system in which the sun replaced the earth as the center of the solar system. His theory was a radical departure from the status quo and became a landmark in the history of modern science that is now known as the Copernican Revolution. Thus, any theory that is considered similarly radical is often referred to as "Copernican" or as a "Copernican revolution."

encounters with the resurrected Christ, they believed Him to be a gardener (John 20:15), a ghost (Luke 24:37), and a mere traveler on the road to Emmaus (Luke 24:13-16). These gross and rather comical misinterpretations were only resolved by further appearances of Christ and through His careful exposition of the Law and the Prophets (Luke 24:25-27, 44-46). Before the doubt of Thomas could be removed, he considered it necessary to see in Christ's hands the imprint of the nails, put his finger into the wounds, and put his hand in His side (John 20:24-29)! Christ even "reproached them for their unbelief and hardness of heart" (Mark 16:14), and He scolded them as "foolish men who were slow of heart to believe in all that the prophets [had] spoken" (Luke 24:25). These facts hardly substantiate the claim that the disciples were predisposed to believe the resurrection!

Lastly, a specific delusion or hallucination is usually confined to a single individual. To think that the hundreds of people who claimed to be eyewitnesses of the risen Christ all shared the same hallucination is extremely improbable. Furthermore, mass hysteria usually requires the aid of powerful political or religious institutions that hold sway over the masses. However, in the case of Christ's resurrection and the gospel, the powerful institutions of the day were combined in their opposition to the message and did everything in their power to discredit it. The propagators were, for the most part, uneducated and untrained men (Acts 4:13) with no political, religious, or economic power to promote their cause.

A LIE WITHOUT A MOTIVE

An often overlooked, yet extremely convincing argument for the historical reality of the resurrection is the apostles' lifelong dedication to the gospel, regardless of the suffering and loss it imposed upon them. If Christ had not risen and the disciples had simply invented the story, then we should be able to discover a motive for the deception. What did they hope to achieve by propagating the lie? It is a historical fact that the apostles and the great majority of the early disciples died poor, defamed, persecuted, and hated. As the Apostle Paul declared, "We have become as the scum of the world, the dregs of all things" (I Corinthians 4:13), and "If we have hoped in Christ in this life only, we are of all men most to be pitied" (I Corinthians 15:19).

If these men had invented the resurrection story for the typical reasons for which men create such lies and propagate them—wealth, fame, and power—then they would have recanted or denounced the story once they saw that it was not achieving their desired goal. Nevertheless, history proves that most of them chose terrible persecution and even martyrdom over the renouncement of their belief in the gospel or the resurrection of Christ upon which it is founded. The only explanation for such tenacity and persistence in the face of such suffering and death is that the resurrection story is true—a historical reality—and that the apostles and other Christians were simply communicating what they had truly witnessed. As the Apostle John wrote, "What we have seen and heard we proclaim to you also" (I John 1:3).

Another important factor to calculate into the equation is the use of women as witnesses. In the time and culture of the New Testament, women were not considered legitimate witnesses in legal proceedings. Nevertheless, in all four Gospels, women take a prominent role as the "first witnesses" to the resurrection of Jesus Christ (Matthew 28:1-10; Mark 16:1-8; Luke 24:1-12; John 20:1-18). Mary Magdalene was the first person to see the Lord after the resurrection, and she was also the first to bear witness of His resurrection to others. In fact, she is portrayed as something of a heroine in that she believed and obeyed in the face of the apostles' unbelief (Mark 16:9-11; John 20:11-18). The women who had accompanied Mary Magdalene to the tomb on Sunday morning were the next to see the Lord, and they were the first to actually be commissioned by Him to take the news to others (Matthew 28:8-10). If the writers of the New Testament had been attempting to deceive the masses, they would not have used women as their primary witnesses; rather, they would have selected men, who would have been much more credible in the eyes of others.

THE TRANSFORMATION OF THE DISCIPLES

One of the greatest hurdles that the skeptic must overcome in his denial of the resurrection of Jesus Christ is the obvious transformation of the disciples. If the resurrection is not a historical reality—or worse, if it is a hoax—then the seemingly miraculous transformation that occurred in the character and deeds of the apostles and the other eyewitnesses is inexplicable.

Prior to the resurrection, the disciples were timid, fearful, and driven by self-preservation. During the arrest of Jesus, they abandoned Him (Matthew 26:56); during the trial, they denied Him (Matthew 26:69-75); and for three days after His death, they hid themselves in unbelief (Mark 16:14; John 20:19) and were engulfed in despair (Luke 24:17). The women among them showed far greater moral fortitude and hope than the very men who had been personally commissioned by Christ to be His apostles! It was the women who went to the tomb on Sunday morning while the men cowered in the upper room. It was the women who first believed and proclaimed the resurrection while the men were muted by doubt.

However, after the resurrection, these same men were transformed into valiant and indomitable defenders of the faith. From the book of Acts, we learn that they stood against the world and "turned [it] upside down" with the message of the gospel and the resurrection of Jesus Christ (Acts 17:6 KJV/NKJV/ESV). When the most powerful religious and political institutions among Jews or Gentiles "commanded them not to speak or teach at all in the name of Jesus" (Acts 4:18), they defied their authority with unflinching commitment to Christ's person and message. This is evident in Peter and John's declaration to the Sanhedrin in Acts 4:19-20:

> Whether it is right in the sight of God to give heed to you rather than to God, you be the judge; for we cannot stop speaking about what we have seen and heard.

Although they were threatened, beaten, imprisoned, and martyred, the disciples of Christ refused to deny or cease from proclaiming what they had "seen and heard" (I John 1:1, 3). These men and women, emboldened by the truth of the resurrection of Jesus, spread the gospel throughout the entire known world in a single generation (Colossians 1:5-6). They had no political, religious, or economic power; and they had no academic credentials; yet still they changed the world to a degree that no political or military machine has ever equaled. If Christ had not risen, how could this be explained? How could the success of their mission be understood? R.A. Torrey writes:

> Something tremendous must have happened to account for such a radical and astounding moral transformation as this. Nothing short of the fact of the resurrection, of their having seen the risen Lord, will explain it.[18]

THE CONVERSION OF ENEMIES

The radical transformation of the followers of Jesus Christ after His resurrection is not the skeptic's only problem. He must also explain the subsequent conversion of those who opposed

---

[18] *The Bible and Its Christ* (Old Tappan, N.J.: Fleming H. Revell, n.d.), p.92.

Jesus and persecuted the movement that followed Him. Apart from the resurrection, how could Christianity have impacted some of its earliest and greatest opponents—especially the half brothers of Jesus and the infamous Saul of Tarsus?

The Scriptures clearly state that during Jesus' life and ministry, neither James nor Jude (Jesus' half brothers) believed in Him but were openly antagonistic toward His person and ministry (John 7:3-5). In fact, Jesus' family once traveled from Nazareth to Capernaum in order to take custody of Him because they thought He had "lost His senses" (Mark 3:21). However, after the resurrection, both brothers were radically converted and became leaders in the early church.[19] Their devotion to Christ and submission to His lordship is seen in the introduction to their epistles, where they refer to themselves as bondservants of the Lord Jesus Christ (James 1:1; Jude 1). They had been transformed from unbelieving antagonists into faithful bondservants who were willing to submit their lives to His lordship. How was such a transformation possible apart from accepting the testimony of Scripture? They had seen the risen Christ (I Corinthians 15:7)!

Another enemy of the early church whose conversion adds weight to the apostolic proclamation of the resurrection is Saul of Tarsus (later known as the Apostle Paul). In the book of Acts and by his own accounts, Saul stands out as the greatest and fiercest enemy of primitive Christianity. In his ignorance and unbelief, he saw Jesus of Nazareth as nothing more than an impostor and a blasphemer, and he thought that all who followed Him were worthy of imprisonment and death (I Timothy 1:13). We first see him in the book of Acts as he gives his hearty approval to the martyrdom of Stephen (Acts 7:58; 8:1). Afterwards, he goes to the high priest, "breathing threats and murder against the disciples of the Lord" (9:1), and asks for letters so that "if he found any belonging to the Way, both men and women, he might bring them bound to Jerusalem" (9:2). However, on the road to Damascus, Saul is radically transformed—he becomes convinced that Jesus is the Messiah of Israel! He receives baptism in His name and immediately begins to proclaim Jesus in the synagogues, saying, "He is the Son of God" (9:18-20). His fellow Jews respond in amazement, saying:

> Is this not he who in Jerusalem destroyed those who called on this name, and who had come here for the purpose of bringing them bound before the chief priests? (Acts 9:21)

After these events, the news quickly spread to all the churches of Judea that he who once had persecuted and tried to destroy the faith was now preaching and proclaiming that same faith (Galatians 1:22-23)! However, Saul had been such a violent adversary to the church that no believer dared associate with him. All were afraid of him until Barnabas brought him to the apostles and confirmed his testimony (Acts 9:26-27). In this way, Saul of Tarsus, the greatest enemy of the Christian faith, became its greatest defender and propagator. William Neil writes:

> What is beyond question historically is that the fanatical oppressor of the Nazarenes, who left Jerusalem "breathing threats and murder," entered Damascus mentally shattered and physically blinded and became on his recovery the foremost protagonist of the beliefs he set out to extirpate [*i.e.* destroy].[20]

---

[19] James (James 1:1; Acts 1:14; 12:17; 15:13ff; I Corinthians 9:5; 15:7; Galatians 1:19; 2:9) and Jude (Jude 1; Acts 1:14; I Corinthians 9:5).

[20] *New Century Bible Commentary – The Acts of the Apostles*, p.128.

Because the skeptic cannot deny the historical realities of Saul's conversion and radically transformed life, he is obliged to offer a reasonable explanation for it. After two thousand years, the church is still waiting!

THE MULTITUDES THROUGHOUT HISTORY

In the first year of Christianity, the respected Pharisee Gamaliel addressed the Sanhedrin with great wisdom regarding the followers of Jesus. It is worth quoting:

> *Men of Israel, take care what you propose to do with these men. For some time ago Theudas rose up, claiming to be somebody, and a group of about four hundred men joined up with him. But he was killed, and all who followed him were dispersed and came to nothing. After this man, Judas of Galilee rose up in the days of the census and drew away some people after him; he too perished, and all those who followed him were scattered. So in the present case, I say to you, stay away from these men and let them alone, for if this plan or action is of men, it will be overthrown; but if it is of God, you will not be able to overthrow them; or else you may even be found fighting against God. (Acts 5:35-39)*

Prior to the coming of Jesus Christ, two false messiahs had appeared to the nation of Israel, and each had drawn a following. Yet after their deaths, their followers were quickly dispersed, and nothing was ever heard of their movements again. Therefore, Gamaliel reasoned that if Jesus of Nazareth were just a man and His resurrection a hoax, then the same fate would befall His followers. However, Gamaliel also wisely concluded that if the resurrection story were true, then Jesus was the Messiah, the movement would continue, and those who opposed it would be fighting against God. The last two thousand years of history seem to have confirmed Gamaliel's argument.

One of the greatest proofs of the resurrection of Jesus Christ is the continuation of the Christian faith throughout history and throughout the nations, tribes, and peoples of the world. Since the resurrection, hundreds of millions of people have testified to having a personal relationship with Jesus Christ and have claimed that He has dramatically changed the course of their lives. It is important to note that this group of people is not confined to any specific ethnic, political, economic, or academic sub-group; rather, it includes individuals from every ethnicity, economic class, and academic level. The early church was made up of individuals who would have never come together in any other circumstance. There were Greeks and Jews, circumcised and uncircumcised, barbarians, Scythians, slaves, and freemen; but Christ was all and in all (Colossians 3:11). The same may be said of Christianity today.

It is also important to note that a countless multitude of men, women, and children who have followed Christ have done so at great personal sacrifice. Some statisticians estimate that the number of martyrs has reached more than fifty million believers. Others claim that this number is much higher.

All of this evidence unrelentingly leads us to several thought-provoking questions. What is the rationale behind such devotion and sacrifice? What is the explanation for the endurance of the church despite the countless enemies who have vowed to exterminate it? It does cause one to think that something truly did happen on that Sunday morning when the stone was found rolled away!

Chapter 24: The Nature of Christ's Resurrection

Having considered the historicity of Christ's resurrection, it is now important to examine its meaning in light of the Scriptures. What was the nature of the resurrection? The English word "resurrection" comes from the Latin verb **resurgere** [**re** = again + **surgere** = to rise]. In the New Testament, it is derived from the Greek noun **anástasis** [**aná** = up, again + **stásis** = stand].

CHRIST'S RESURRECTION WAS NOT MERELY A REVIVIFICATION

In the Old Testament, the son of the widow of Zarephath (I Kings 17:17-24) and the Shunammite's son (II Kings 4:18-37) were supernaturally resurrected. The New Testament teaches that Lazarus was resurrected (John 11:23-25, 43-44), along with Jairus's daughter (Mark 5:41-42; Luke 8:54-55), a young man from Nain (Luke 7:14-15), Tabitha (Acts 9:36-43), and Eutychus (Acts 20:7-12). It is important to note that all of these were revived from the dead, but they all were still subject to death—they would die again. Christ's resurrection was different in that He died once for sin but lives forevermore, never to die again. As He declared in Revelation 1:18: "[I am] the living One; and I was dead, and behold, I am alive forevermore…"

CHRIST'S RESURRECTION WAS A BODILY RESURRECTION

It is the plain teaching of Scripture and of all orthodox Christianity that Christ's resurrection was a bodily resurrection. The very same body that was crucified, wrapped in burial cloth, and placed in the tomb was raised on the third day according to the Scriptures. Although this raised body was the very same that had died, it also had many differences. It was sown in weakness, but raised in power.

1. It is important to establish what is meant by the term "resurrection." The Scriptures teach that the resurrection of Jesus was not merely spiritual, but material, physical, and corporeal. The actual flesh-and-bone body of Jesus was resurrected. What do we learn about this truth from Luke 24:36-43? Read the text, and then answer the following questions.

    a. *How should verses 36-37 be interpreted? Was there a supernatural element to Christ's entrance? What does this tell us about His resurrection body?*

    _____

    _____

    _____

_____

_____

NOTES: According to John 20:19, the disciples were gathered behind "shut" doors for fear of the Jews. This fact, coupled with the frightened reaction of the disciples, indicates that Jesus came into the room by supernatural means and that His resurrected body was of a different order. This truth is also seen in Jesus' encounter with the two disciples on the road to Emmaus, where He "vanished from their sight" (Luke 24:31). The terms "startled" and "frightened" come from the Greek words **_ptoéō_** and **_émphobos_**. Both terms denote a very strong fear. They thought that they were seeing a disembodied spirit.

b. _According to verses 39-40, what proof did Jesus give to convince His disciples that He was not a spirit? What does this teach us about His resurrected body?_

_____

_____

_____

_____

_____

NOTES: Jesus makes two important declarations regarding His resurrected body: (1) that He had flesh and bones; and (2) that He was not a disembodied spirit, as they had first supposed. To give further evidence, Jesus invited His disciples to observe and even touch His hands and feet. The fact that Christ's resurrected body still bore the scars of the crucifixion proved that it was indeed the same body that was crucified. The fact that Christ went to such lengths to prove that He was not a mere spirit indicates the extreme importance of the doctrine of His bodily resurrection.

c. _What further evidence did Jesus give in verses 41-43 to prove to the disciples that He was not a spirit? What does this teach us about His resurrected body?_

_____

_____

_____

NOTES: The sudden appearance of Jesus in their midst caused great amazement. They were uncertain about what they were seeing and what was happening among them. When the patriarch Jacob was told that his son Joseph was alive, the Scriptures declare that he responded in a similar manner: "He was stunned, for he did not believe them" (Genesis 45:26). Because of their unbelief, Christ went to even greater lengths to prove that His body, though transformed in marvelous ways, was still the same real body that had hung on the cross—He asked them for a piece of fish and ate it before their very eyes.

2. In John 20:19-23, we are given John's account of Christ's appearance to the disciples at a time when Thomas was not present. In the verses that follow (vv.24-29), we are given the account of Christ's appearance to all of the disciples, including Thomas. Read the text, and then answer the following questions.

   a. *According to verses 24-25, what was Thomas's reaction when the other disciples declared to him that they had seen the Lord? Why is Thomas's reaction significant?*

   _____

   _____

   _____

   _____

   _____

   NOTES: Thomas's reaction was one of doubt or disbelief. This proves that the disciples were not men who expected Christ to rise again; therefore, they could not have simply imagined the resurrection story as something they hoped to be true, for they clearly did not initially believe it themselves! It also shows that they were not gullible men who could be led to believe without sufficient proof. Even after reports of Christ's resurrection began to surface, the disciples still did not believe. Luke records that the news of Christ's resurrection "appeared to them as nonsense" (Luke 24:9-11), and Mark writes that they "refused to believe it" (Mark 16:11).

   b. *In verse 26, we learn that Jesus appeared a second time to the disciples, this time while Thomas was present. According to verses 27-28, what did Jesus command Thomas to do, and what was Thomas's reaction? What does this teach us about both the certainty and the nature of Christ's resurrection?*

   _____

   _____

_____

_____

_____

NOTES: The fact that Thomas was commanded to examine the physical body of Jesus indicates at least two things: (1) Thomas was not seeing a hallucination, but a real person standing before him; and (2) Jesus was resurrected with the same body that had been crucified—it bore the scars of the crucifixion and of the impalement by the lance. Christ's appearance in the same body which had been crucified resulted in the transformation of Thomas's faith. He went from believing that Jesus was a martyred prophet to proclaiming Him as the Lord and God of creation!

3. In I Corinthians 15:42-44, the Apostle Paul sets forth the differences between a mortal human body and the same body after the resurrection. In this text, we can learn several truths about the differences between Christ's earthly body prior to His death and His resurrected body. Fill in the blanks below according to the texts given.

   a. *It was sown a P_____ body and raised an I_____ body (v.42).* The word "perishable" comes from the Greek phrase **en phthorá**, which is literally translated, "in corruption." Christ's earthly body was subject to aging, deterioration, and death. The word "imperishable" comes from the Greek word **aphtharsía**, which refers to that which is not subject to corruption. Christ's resurrected body was not subject to deterioration or death; rather, it was fit for eternity.

   b. *It was sown in D_____ and raised in G_____ (v.43).* The word "dishonor" is translated from the Greek word **atimía**, which denotes dishonor or shame. In His earthly ministry, Christ had "no stately form or majesty" (Isaiah 53:2); and on the cross, He suffered the greatest of all humiliations (Philippians 2:8). However, His body was raised in glory. The word comes from the Greek word **dóxa**, which denotes glory, honor, and majesty.

   c. *It was sown in W_____ and raised in P_____ (v.43).* The word "weakness" comes from the Greek word **asthéneia**, which may also be translated, "frailty." In the incarnation, Christ took upon Himself a body that was subject to all the infirmities of fallen man—hunger, thirst, pain, sickness, agony, and death (Romans 8:3). However, His body was raised in power. The word "power" comes from the Greek word **dúnamis**, which denotes power, might, and strength. The writer of Hebrews declares that Christ now possesses "the power of an indestructible life" (Hebrews 7:16).

   d. *It was sown a N_____ body and raised a S_____ body (v.44).* The word "natural" comes from the Greek word **psuchikós**, which refers to that which pertains to the natural realm and is characterized by weakness, decay, and death. The word "spiritual" comes from the Greek word **pneumatikós**, which denotes that which pertains to the heavenly realm and is marked by power and eternality. Christ's resurrected body is set in contrast to the "natural body." It is important to note

NOTES: In verses 9 and 10, Luke writes that the disciples "were looking on" and "were gazing intently into the sky." Both phrases refer to the eyewitness accounts that Luke used as sources for his Gospel. The phrase "gazing intently" comes from the Greek word **atenízō**, which means, "to fix one's eyes on, look straight at, or stare." The same word is used in Luke 4:20, when the Scriptures declare that "the eyes of all in the synagogue were fixed [or fastened] on Him [Jesus]." The disciples did not simply catch a momentary glance of something they misinterpreted as Jesus. They had ample time to evaluate the event, even as they were witnessing it. In verse 11, the disciples are mildly rebuked by the angels because they continued looking up to the sky even after Jesus had departed. Again, this demonstrates how thoroughly they witnessed the event. Skeptics have attempted to discredit Luke's account by pointing out that his use of the phrase "was lifted up" is incompatible with our knowledge of the universe. Such criticism is unnecessary. Luke uses the same terminology that modern-day scientists use to describe the "lifting up" of a rocket.

3. It is clear that the New Testament writers saw the ascension of Jesus as a historical event. Forty days after the resurrection, Jesus ascended from the earth, but to where did He ascend? What do the following Scriptures teach us?

   a. *He was C_____ U_____ into heaven (Luke 24:51).* The phrase "carried up" comes from the Greek word **anaphérō**, which means, "to carry, bear, or bring up." In this context, the word "heaven" [Greek: **ouranós**] refers to the very abode of God. Matthew Henry writes, "He was carried up into heaven; not by force, but by his own act and deed… There was no need of a chariot of fire or horses of fire; He knew the way."[21]

   b. *He P_____ T_____ the heavens (Hebrews 4:14).* The phrase "passed through" comes from the Greek word **diérchomai**, which means, "to go or pass through, to walk or journey through a place." Christ passed through all the heavens until He reached the highest place, the very presence of God.

   c. *He A_____ F_____ A_____ all the heavens (Ephesians 4:10).* The word "ascended" comes from the Greek word **anabaínō**, which means, "to ascend, climb up, or rise." Christ ascended to the highest place in all the heavens.

   d. *He was T_____ U_____ in G_____ (I Timothy 3:16).* The phrase "taken up" comes from the Greek word **analambánō**, which means, "to take or receive up." Christ ascended to the glorious abode of God. He was taken up to this place and well-received.

   e. *He was received up into heaven and sat down at the R_____ hand of God (Mark 16:19).* The phrase "received up" comes from the Greek word **analambánō** (see definition above). Matthew Henry writes, "He had not only an admission, but an abundant entrance into His kingdom."[22] Having ascended, Christ "sat down at the right

---

[21] *Matthew Henry Commentary*, Vol.5, p.846
[22] *Matthew Henry Commentary*, Vol.5, p.572

hand of God." There is no place of greater exaltation than at God's right hand, the place of His favor and authority.

f. *He went to the F_____ (John 14:28).* Christ returned to His greatest love, to the One for whom He did this great work of redemption—the Father. He had pleased the Father in all things, and now He returned home with His Father's unreserved approval.

g. *He A_____ to where He was B_____ (John 6:62).* The word "ascended" comes from the Greek word **anabaínō**, which means, "to ascend, climb up, or rise." Two things are taught in this text: (1) the Son's eternal glory prior to His incarnation; and (2) the Son's return to His previous exalted state, this time as the God-Man.

THE EXALTATION

The Scriptures teach that Jesus Christ not only ascended to heaven, but that He also was exalted to the position of highest honor and authority at the very right hand of God. It is extremely important to note that this exaltation was not a "new" or "strange" experience for the Son of God. The Scriptures clearly teach that He was glorified together with the Father and shared His Father's glory before the world was (John 17:5). The uniqueness of the Son's return to exaltation is found in this: He who is now exalted at the right hand of the Father is both God and Man. In the incarnation, the Son divested Himself of the honors and rights (though not the essence) of His deity, took upon Himself our humanity, and was obedient to the Father's will even to the point of death on a cross. For this reason, He "won" the right to sit down at the right hand of God. The One who has been crowned with glory and honor on the very throne of God is both God and Man. The exalted Savior and King is one with God and one with His people.

1. In Isaiah 52:13-14 is found a powerful prophecy concerning the Messiah's exaltation after suffering for the sins of His people. Summarize the major truths of the text.

_____

_____

_____

_____

_____

NOTES: The phrase "My servant" is a reference to the Messiah. God has had only one true Servant—His Son Jesus Christ. The word "prosper" comes from the Hebrew word **sakal**, which indicates prosperity or success. It denotes God's favor or blessing and is often the reward for obedience (Joshua 1:8). There has never been anyone as obedient or pleasing to God as His Son—He was obedient to the point of death on a cross (v.14; see also Philippians 2:8). Therefore, there would be no one more highly exalted or lifted up.

2. In Isaiah 53:10-12 is found another detailed prophecy concerning the coming Messiah, His suffering, and His glorious exaltation. Summarize in your own words what each verse communicates to us about the Son's ultimate exaltation at the right hand of God.

a. *He will see His offspring, He will prolong His days, and the good pleasure of the Lord will prosper in His hand (v.10).*

NOTES: As a result of His obedience, the Son would be resurrected and live forever ("He will prolong His days"); He would be given a spiritual offspring ("He will see His offspring"); and God's will or "good pleasure" would "prosper" perfectly through Him.

b. *As a result of the anguish of His soul, He will see it and be satisfied (v.11).*

NOTES: The word "anguish" comes from the Hebrew word `amal, which denotes toil, trouble, travail, grievous labor, vexation, misery, and pain. The Messiah would suffer these things to the very depth of His being (physically, emotionally, mentally, and spiritually). However, as a result of His anguish, many would be justified; and He would be satisfied with His reward. The word "satisfied" comes from the Hebrew word **saba**, which means, "to be satisfied, sated, or fulfilled to the point of excess."

c. *Therefore, I will allot Him a portion with the great, and He will divide the booty with the strong (v.12).*

NOTES: God's exaltation and reward would be the fruit of the Messiah's obedience unto death, even death on a cross. The references to the allotting of portions and the dividing of booty portray Calvary as a great conquest or military victory. Christ the Victor is given the spoils of His victory.

3. In Philippians 2:6-11 is found one of the most important passages in all of Scripture regarding the humiliation and exaltation of the Son of God. Read the text several times until you are familiar with its contents, and then write your own commentary on each of the following portions. What was Christ's reward for His voluntary humiliation?

a. *For this reason also, God highly exalted Him, and bestowed on Him the name which is above every name (v.9).*

_____

_____

_____

_____

_____

_____

_____

NOTES: The phrase, "for this reason," is important. God exalted Jesus above every name "because of" or "on account of" [Greek: *dió*] His voluntary submission to God, which He demonstrated in His incarnation, obedience, and atoning death. Upon His ascension into heaven, the Son of God and Son of Man took the place that He had possessed before the foundation of the world. He is exalted not only by divine right, but also as a reward for His perfect obedience as a Man. The phrase "highly exalted" comes from the Greek word *huperupsóō*, which denotes the act of exalting one to the highest rank and power. The word "bestowed" comes from the Greek word *charízomai*, which denotes giving something pleasant or agreeable to another and doing so graciously and freely. The phrase, "above every name," refers to the Son's exalted state over every created being in heaven and on earth.

b. *So that at the name of Jesus every knee will bow, of those who are in heaven and on earth and under the earth, and that every tongue will confess that Jesus Christ is Lord, to the glory of God the Father (vv.10-11).*

_____

_____

_____

_____

_____

_____

_____

_____

NOTES: In Isaiah 45:23, God declares the following concerning Himself: "I have sworn by Myself, the word has gone forth from My mouth in righteousness and will not turn back, that to Me every knee will bow, every tongue will swear allegiance." That this text is applied to Christ is great proof of His deity. The bowing of the knee represents the recognition of worth, the giving of honor, and submission to authority. This text communicates two great truths. First, Christ is worthy of all honor and submission. Second, there is coming a day when all creation will recognize and acknowledge Christ as Lord.

4. The following New Testament texts give us some important insight into Christ's exaltation and its purpose. Write your thoughts on each text.

   a. *Hebrews 1:3*

   _____

   _____

   _____

   _____

   _____

NOTES: The word "purification" comes from the Greek word **katharismós**, which may also be translated, "cleansing." It is a reference to Christ's atoning work on Calvary whereby His people have been purified from sin. The phrase, "Majesty on high," is a reference to God and His greatness. The fact that Christ has sat down at the right hand of God demonstrates that He has been given the place of highest honor and favor, a place and rank equal with God.

b. *Hebrews 2:9*

_____

_____

_____

_____

NOTES: Again, Christ's humiliation and atoning death are viewed as a cause or basis for His exaltation. The writer of Hebrews could not have chosen a more majestic phrase than "crowned with glory and honor." However, even this does not begin to describe the glory that has been bestowed upon Christ.

c. *Revelation 3:21*

_____

_____

_____

_____

NOTES: The word "overcome" comes from the Greek word **nikáō**, which means, "to conquer" or "to be victorious." Christ's submission to the Father's will and His perfect obedience were necessary precursors to His exaltation. In His obedience and submission, Christ overcame sin, Satan, and death. His exaltation is portrayed as a reward for His obedience.

Chapter 28: Our Exalted Savior

The eternal Son of God divested Himself of the honors of deity and took upon Himself our humanity. He walked upon this earth and lived a perfect life in unwavering submission to the will of God. According to the foreordained plan of God, He was lifted up and nailed to a Roman cross by the hands of wicked men. On that cross, He bore the sins of His people and suffered the wrath of God in their place. By His death, He satisfied God's justice and made it possible for a just God to forgive the sins of His people and grant them a perfect standing before Him. As a result of His obedience, the incarnate Son was raised from the dead and exalted to the right hand of God as Savior. He alone bears the title of Savior, and in His name alone is salvation found.

The Scriptures declare unapologetically that salvation is found in the name of Jesus Christ alone. There is no other savior, mediator, or means by which a man may obtain forgiveness for his sin and be reconciled to God; this work can only be accomplished through the person of Jesus Christ and His perfect work on Calvary. This is one of the most scandalous truths of Christianity; however, to harbor the slightest compromise of this truth is to deny the Scriptures, diminish the glory of Christ, make void the cross, and drive a dagger into the very heart of the gospel. The only faithful proclamation of the gospel is that which boldly and clearly declares Jesus Christ to be the One and only Savior!

1. In John 14:6, Jesus made a bold declaration about Himself with regard to truth, life, and reconciliation with God. In the mind of Christ, is there any possibility of finding truth, life, or salvation in anyone or anything outside of Himself? Write your thoughts regarding each of the following phrases.

   a. *I am the way...*

   _____

   _____

   _____

   _____

   _____

NOTES: Christ is the "Highway of Holiness" prophesied in Isaiah 35:8 and the "new and living way" spoken of in Hebrews 10:20. He is the only Way upon which man and God meet. There may be many roads that lead to Rome, but there is only one that leads to pardon for sin and a right relationship with God—Jesus Christ.

b. *And the truth...*

_____

_____

_____

_____

NOTES: Christ is more than a teacher of the truth; He *is* the Truth—the greatest manifestation of truth to men and the standard by which all other thoughts, words, and deeds are judged. His person and teaching represent the greatest embodiment of truth ever given to man. Any teaching that contradicts Christ or exalts itself as superior to Christ is false.

c. *And the life...*

_____

_____

_____

_____

NOTES: John begins His Gospel by declaring that, "In Him [*i.e.* the Son] was life, and the life was the Light of men" (1:4). In John 5:26, Jesus taught not only that life was through Him, but also that He had "life in Himself." From the beginning, the Son has been the Mediator of all life to men, both physically and spiritually. He is the True Vine, who alone brings spiritual life to those who abide in Him (John 15:1-6). Apart from Him, there is no true spirituality.

d. *No one comes to the Father but through Me.*

_____

_____

_____

_____

NOTES: This is the great scandal of the Christian faith. True Christianity is very exclusive in that it admits no one to heaven except through Christ and His atoning work on Calvary. The Old Testament saints were justified by faith in the revelation of God that they had received and in the promises of a future hope through the Messiah. Now that the Messiah has come and has fulfilled all the Old Testament prophecies and promises, salvation is found only in His name and in His work of redemption.

2. To ensure that our interpretation of the words of Jesus is correct, we only need to look to a few bold declarations made in the preaching and writings of the apostles. According to the following Scriptures, how did they interpret the person and saving work of Jesus Christ? Is He *a* savior or *the* Savior?

   a. *Acts 4:12*

   _____

   _____

   _____

   _____

   NOTES: It would hardly be possible for Peter to speak more clearly regarding the uniqueness of Christ and His ability to save. His words are reminiscent of God's great declarations spoken through the prophet Isaiah: "I, even I, am the Lord, and there is no savior besides Me" (Isaiah 43:11); and, "There is no other God besides Me, a righteous God and a Savior; there is none except Me" (Isaiah 45:21b). This is the great banner of Christianity. Every realm of creation may be searched, but none can be found worthy of the title of Savior except the Lamb of God.

   b. *I Corinthians 3:11*

   _____

   _____

   _____

   _____

   NOTES: Throughout the Scriptures, Christ is referred to as the foundation and cornerstone upon which salvation and the church rest (Isaiah 28:16; Matthew 21:42; Acts 4:11;

Ephesians 2:20; II Timothy 2:19; I Peter 2:6). God has laid only one foundation stone, and it is Christ. He alone has God's seal.

   c. *I Timothy 2:5*

_____

_____

_____

_____

NOTES: The doctrine of salvation in Christ alone is as foundational to biblical Christianity as the doctrine of monotheism (*i.e.* the belief in only one God). The word "mediator" comes from the Greek word ***mesítēs***, which denotes an arbitrator or go-between. In our present context, it refers to an arbitrator between God and man. The reference to Jesus as "the man" is not a denial of His deity, but is designed to emphasize His humanity in order to provide comfort for the believer. Our Mediator is like us, and He is not ashamed to call us brothers (Hebrews 2:11).

   d. *I John 5:12*

_____

_____

_____

_____

NOTES: Again, the clarity of this text cannot be questioned. All true spiritual life and any hope of eternal life resulting from a reconciled relationship to God are determined by one's relationship with Christ. "In Christ alone" is the consistent maxim and motto of the writers of the New Testament. A person can disagree with their testimony that Christ is the only Way, but one cannot disagree that it was their testimony!

3. In Acts 5:31 and 11:17-18 are found two important declarations regarding the claim that salvation is found in Christ alone. They prove that Christ is neither simply the Savior of the Jews to the exclusion of the Gentiles nor the Savior of only the Gentiles to the exclusion of the Jews, but that He is God's appointed Savior for all peoples.

a. *In Acts 5:31, what does the Apostle Peter declare regarding Christ's relationship to the Jews?*

_____

_____

_____

_____

NOTES: God's exaltation of Jesus is proof that He is God's appointed Deliverer to bring salvation to His ancient people, the Jews.

b. *According to Acts 11:17-18, what did the Jewish Christians concede after they heard Peter's account of God's saving work among the Gentiles? Is Christ God's appointed Savior to the Jews alone or also to the Gentiles?*

_____

_____

_____

_____

4. In Romans 1:16, the Apostle Paul makes a very important statement regarding the gospel of Jesus Christ as the one and only means of salvation for all people. Consider the text, and write your thoughts.

_____

_____

_____

_____

_____

NOTES: It takes great power [Greek: *dúnamis*] to regenerate the spiritually dead, justify the sinner, and sanctify the unclean. Such power is found in the *gospel alone*, which points to *Christ alone* as the only Savior by whom men can be saved.

Chapter 29: Our Exalted Mediator

The saving work of Christ does not end with His death on the cross; it continues in His exaltation. Christ is the Great High Priest who offered the perfect sacrifice of Himself to satisfy the justice of God and save His people from wrath; but He is also the Great High Priest who stands in heaven on their behalf and lives forever to intercede for them before God. In the incarnation, the Son took upon Himself the humanity of His people so that He might die in their place. The Son now stands in heaven robed in the same humanity now glorified, representing His people before God as their Mediator and Advocate. In the next two chapters, we will look closely at these two roles—Mediator (this chapter) and Advocate (next chapter).

The word "mediator" comes from the Latin verb **mediare**, which means, "to be in the middle." The Greek word for "mediator" is **mesítēs** (derived from the verb **mesiteúō**, meaning, "to bring about agreement"). The following definitions of "mediator" are helpful.

> One who causes or helps parties to come to an agreement, with the implication of guaranteeing the certainty of the arrangement. (*Louw & Nida Greek Lexicon*)

> One that acts between two parties; one who interposes to reconcile two adverse parties; an arbitrator; one who is the medium of communication between two parties, a mid-party. (*Mounce Greek Dictionary*)

Webster defines a mediator as "one who is qualified and able to interpose between two parties in order to reconcile them to one another." In order to be a proper Mediator between God and man, it was necessary that Jesus of Nazareth be both God and Man in one person. He must be fully Man so that He might lay His hand upon man, reveal God to him, and bring him comfort. He must be fully God so that He might lay His hand upon God, be the full revelation of divine majesty, and interpose on man's behalf. It would be the worst sort of blasphemy to ascribe such power to even the most exalted creature. The majestic seraphim that inhabit the very throne room of God would not even venture to claim to be His reflection, much less stretch forth their hands to claim to be His mediator! Splendid as they are, they dare do little more than bow their heads, cover themselves, and cry out that He alone is holy, holy, holy (Isaiah 6:2-3)!

Mediation is a work beyond the ability of any creature. It is an office that belongs only to Christ! He alone qualifies to stand before God on our behalf, because He alone is the fullness of God in bodily form. He is God in the strictest sense, and He also is a Man like us except without sin.

1. Since the fall of Adam, mankind's greatest need has been someone who could represent them before God and act as a mediator. Such a representative was man's only hope for reconciliation with God. This ancient dilemma is clearly portrayed in the book of Job. What was Job's great complaint in Job 9:29-33? Write your thoughts on the following quotes from this passage.

a. *I am accounted wicked, why then should I toil in vain? If I should wash myself with snow and cleanse my hands with lye, yet You would plunge me into the pit, and my own clothes would abhor me (vv.29-31).*

_____

_____

_____

_____

_____

_____

NOTES: Job recognized two very important truths. First, like all men, he was a sinner before God. Second, all his toil to justify himself before God was in vain. In Jeremiah 2:22, God declares, "Although you wash yourself with lye and use much soap, the stain of your iniquity is before Me." This is the dreadful reality of those who understand something of both the holiness of God and their own extreme moral failure. Apart from Christ, His atoning sacrifice, His imputed righteousness, and His perpetual mediation, man is without hope.

b. *For He is not a man as I am that I may answer Him, that we may go to court together (v.32).*

_____

_____

_____

_____

NOTES: Job recognized that God is holy—separated from sinners and beyond the reach of man. This is one of the great "first truths" or "foundational truths" regarding the true knowledge of God. God told Moses, "You cannot see My face, for no man can see Me and live!" (Exodus 33:20). Job recognized this truth. How could he even dare to imagine that he could enter into God's presence? The question remains for Job and us: "How can we approach God?" A mediator is required: One who is comfortable in the very presence of God and One with whom we can find comfort.

c. *There is no umpire between us, who may lay his hand upon us both (v.33).*

_____

_____

_____

_____

_____

NOTES: The word "umpire" is translated from the Hebrew word **yakach**, which refers to an umpire, mediator, or arbitrator. Job recognized his need for a mediator who was qualified to stand between him and God. In I Samuel 2:25, we read, "If one man sins against another, God will mediate for him; but if a man sins against the Lord, who can intercede for him?" This truth is the basis of Job's complaint. The proper Mediator would have to be a Man in order to lay His hand upon Job, but He would also have to be God that He might lay His hand upon God. Both of these qualifications are met in Jesus. He is a Man who can sympathize with our weaknesses; and He is also the Son of God who has passed through the heavens and is seated at the right hand of God, daily making intercession on behalf of His people.

2. The Scriptures declare that the greatest need of all men is that of a mediator to stand between them and God. Scripture also teaches that God has met this need in the person of Jesus Christ. What does I Timothy 2:5 tell us about this truth?

_____

_____

_____

_____

_____

NOTES: The declaration of "one God" is the great confession of Israel and the church (Deuteronomy 6:4). To deny that Christ is the **only** mediator is equal to denying that the God of the Scriptures is the **only** God. As stated above, the word "mediator" comes from the Greek word **mesítēs**, which refers to a mediator or intermediary. It denotes one who intervenes between two parties in order to make or restore peace, to form a treaty, or to ratify a covenant. By mentioning the two parties ("God and man") in a conjunctive relationship, Paul demonstrates the unique requirements of the Mediator. He must possess the fullness of deity in order to draw near to God and be our Advocate (I John 2:1). However, He must also be fully human that He might stand in our legally rightful place and make atonement for our sin, that He might not overpower us with His majesty, that He might make God known to us, and that He might sympathize with our weaknesses (Hebrews 4:15). By placing "man" before "Christ Jesus," the Apostle Paul is not intending to deny or even diminish Christ's deity; rather, he is simply giving greater emphasis to Christ's humanity in His role as the Mediator through whom frail men can draw near to God. Without denying Christ's deity, Paul is intent on demonstrating that Christ is like us.

3. The Scriptures teach that Jesus Christ is uniquely qualified to be the Mediator between God and man. As the God-Man, He is able to represent both parties and bring about reconciliation between them. What does Hebrews 4:15-16 teach us about this truth?

    a. *For we do not have a high priest who cannot sympathize with our weaknesses, but One who has been tempted in all things as we are, yet without sin (v.15).*

    _____

    _____

    _____

    _____

    _____

    NOTES: Christ is the Great High Priest, the ultimate and greater fulfillment of the Levitical high priesthood (Hebrews 4:14). The word "sympathize" is translated from the Greek word **sumpathéō** [**sún** = with + **páschō** = suffer], which means, "to be affected with the same feelings or weaknesses of another." The KJV translates it, "touched with the feeling of our infirmities." The word "weaknesses" is translated from the Greek word **asthéneia** [**a** = no + **sthénos** = strength], which denotes weakness, infirmity, feebleness, incapacity, or inability. The Scriptures teach that Christ came in the likeness of sinful flesh (Romans 8:3). This does not mean that His body was sinful, but only that it was subject to all the frailties of fallen humanity. Christ's body was not a glorious, prefall, Adamic body as is often and erroneously supposed. The word "tempted" comes from the Greek word **peirázō**. Positively, the word refers to trying or testing for the purpose of determining the quality of something. Negatively, it refers to the act of enticing so as to cause one to sin. The latter meaning is clearly intended here. Christ was tempted in all things by the devil and every fallen instrument (man and demon) at his disposal. It is important to note that the verb **peirázō** appears in the perfect tense. Christ has already been fully and completely tempted in all things as we are. This does not mean that we have faced or will face every temptation imaginable, but that **He has**. Therefore, He is able to help us in **all** our circumstances. There is no temptation that He has not already faced and overcome. For this reason, He is said to be "without sin." This is possibly the most astounding characteristic of the Man Jesus of Nazareth—He was entirely without sin! Christ is the sole person among all of humanity about whom this claim can be made.

b. *Therefore let us draw near with confidence to the throne of grace, so that we may receive mercy and find grace to help in time of need (v.16).*

_____

_____

_____

_____

_____

_____

NOTES: The word "confidence" comes from the Greek word **parrhēsías**, which denotes openness, freedom, full assurance, and even boldness. Because Christ truly entered into our fallen human reality, because He was tempted in all things, because He has done away with our sin through Calvary, and because He is truly sympathetic to our plight, we may now draw near with confidence! The Throne of Judgment has been transformed into a Throne of Grace. Since Christ came in the likeness of sinful flesh (Romans 8:3) and was tempted in all things, yet without sin, He is uniquely qualified to sympathize with our weakness and to provide us with the exact kind and measure of aid we need to face every test of our faith and every temptation of the devil.

Chapter 30: Our Exalted Advocate

In His role as Mediator, Christ acts as the Advocate for His people. The word "advocate" comes from the Latin word **advocatus** [**ad** = to, toward + **vocare** = to call] and refers to one who is called to another in order to plead their case or cause. In the Greek, the word translated as "advocate" is **paráklētos**. It refers to someone summoned or called to another's side to help or to plead another's cause before a judge or king. The word may also be translated, "pleader," "defender," "counsel for defense," or "lawyer." Jesus Christ is the Advocate for His people, and He lives forever to make intercession before the throne of God on their behalf. One of the best explanations of Christ's role as Advocate is found in the Westminster Larger Catechism, Question 55:

> **Question:** How does Christ make intercession?
>
> **Answer:** Christ makes intercession by His appearing in our nature continually before the Father in heaven in the merit of His obedience and sacrifice on earth; declaring His will to have it applied to all believers; answering all accusations against them; and procuring [*i.e.* obtaining or acquiring] for them quiet of conscience (notwithstanding daily failings), access with boldness to the throne of grace, and acceptance of their persons and services [to God].

Before we continue with our study of the Scriptures, it is important to point out that the truth of Christ's continuous intercession for His people does not mean that He is on His knees before the throne of God begging for mercy on our behalf. He intercedes as One seated at the very right hand of God, as One who is omniscient and knows every need of His people, as One who has all authority to speak on their behalf, and as One who annuls every accusation against them. The following quotes from J. I. Packer (1926-), William Ames (1576-1633), and Louis Berkhof (1873-1957) are helpful:

> The essence of Christ's intercession is intervention in our interest (from His throne) rather than supplication on our behalf (as if His position were one of sympathy without status or authority).[23]

> His kingly priesthood is the pleading of our cause, not by suffering and humble supplication on bended knee, as it were, but by gloriously bringing to mind the things which He did and suffered.[24]

> Christ presents Himself before God as our representative. His perfect manhood, His official character, and His finished work plead for us before the throne of God. All that the Son of God as incarnate is, and all that He did on earth, He is and did for us; so that God can regard us with all the favor which is due to Him. His presence, therefore, is a perpetual and prevailing intercession with God in behalf of His people, and secures for them all the benefits of His redemption.[25]

---

[23] J. I. Packer, *Concise Theology*, p.128
[24] William Ames, *The Marrow of Theology*, p.148
[25] Louis Berkhof, *Systematic Theology*, Vol.2, p.593

1. Hebrews 9:24 communicates the power and efficacy of Christ's intercessory ministry on behalf of His people. According to this text, how does Christ's ministry differ from that of the priests of the Old Covenant? How near is Christ to God? How does this prove the power of His advocacy on behalf of His people?

_____

_____

_____

_____

_____

_____

NOTES: The priests in the Old Testament entered yearly into an earthly temple to offer animal sacrifices and to intercede on behalf of the people. Having offered Himself once and for all as a sacrifice of infinite value, Christ entered permanently into the very throne room of God and now lives to make intercession to God on our behalf.

2. I John 2:1-2 is one of the most important texts in all of Scripture regarding Christ's work as Advocate. Read the text until you are familiar with its contents, and then write your thoughts on each of the following phrases.

    a. *My little children, I am writing these things to you so that you may not sin (v.1).*

    _____

    _____

    _____

    _____

    _____

NOTES: The fact that we have an Advocate before the Father should not make us apathetic about holiness or careless about sin. On the contrary, it should motivate us to obedience because of the great work Christ has done for us.

b. *And if anyone sins, we have an Advocate with the Father, Jesus Christ the righteous (v.1).*

_____

_____

_____

_____

_____

NOTES: Even the most mature Christian is still subject to moral weakness and sin. Therefore, it is our great consolation that we have an Advocate with the Father. The word "advocate" comes from the Greek word ***paráklētos***, which denotes a "helper" or one who is called to speak on another's behalf. Jesus is uniquely qualified for this role because He is righteous and worthy to stand before God.

c. *And He Himself is the propitiation for our sins; and not for ours only, but also for those of the whole world (v.2).*

_____

_____

_____

_____

NOTES: The word "propitiation" comes from the Greek word ***hilasmós***, which indicates appeasement or satisfaction; it refers to a sacrifice given to appease an offended party. Christ is our propitiation in that He offered His life in our place as a sacrifice for sin. His sacrifice satisfied the demands of God's justice against us and appeased His wrath. The sacrifice of Christ was not limited to the Jews or any one people group, but encompasses every tribe and tongue and people and nation (Revelation 5:9).

3. In Romans 8:33-34, we find another important Scripture passage regarding Christ's intercessory ministry. According to this text, what is the result of Christ's saving work and intercessory ministry?

_____

_____

_____

_____

_____

NOTES: The questions, "Who will bring a charge against God's elect?" and "Who is the one who condemns?" are one and the same. It is as though God were issuing a challenge to every being in the universe, including Satan himself. The reason why no charge or condemnation can be brought against God's people is two-fold. First, God has justified His people or given them a perfect legal standing before Him. This was accomplished through the perfect life that Christ lived and the death that He died on behalf of His people. Second, Christ now sits at the right hand of God as His people's Intercessor and Defender.

4. In Hebrews 7:23-25, the writer describes not only the power and efficacy of Christ's intercessory ministry but also its permanence. Summarize the text in your own words.

_____

_____

_____

_____

_____

NOTES: This text leaves little to be explained. By the power of Christ's endless life, He is able to save forever those who draw near to God through Him. The Reformer Francis Turretin wrote that Christ appears in heaven as a Lamb that was "standing as if slain" (Revelation 5:6) because "His blood is ever fresh and living—of eternal virtue and efficacy."[26]

5. Although the Scriptures do not reveal the exact nature of Christ's heavenly intercession before the throne of God, some clues may be found in His "High Priestly Prayer" that He prayed on behalf of His disciples during His earthly ministry (John 17:1-26). Below is a list of the petitions that Christ made for His people in that prayer. Match each petition with its corresponding text.

_____	*John 17:11-12*	a.	*Christ intercedes for the future glorification of His people.*
_____	*John 17:13*	b.	*Christ intercedes for the unity of His people.*
_____	*John 17:15*	c.	*Christ intercedes for the sanctification of His people.*
_____	*John 17:17-19*	d.	*Christ intercedes for the protection of His people from all satanic forces (see also Luke 22:32).*
_____	*John 17:21-23*	e.	*Christ intercedes for the perseverance of His people.*
_____	*John 17:24*	f.	*Christ intercedes for the joy of His people.*

---

[26] *Institutes of Elenctic Theology*, Vol.2, p.485

Chapter 31: Christ the King

The Scriptures teach that the Son of God emptied Himself of His divine glory and privileges, took up our lowly humanity, and was scandalously crucified on a Roman cross as a sacrifice for sin. The Scriptures also teach that this same Jesus was raised from the dead, taken up into heaven, and exalted to the very throne of God as the King of kings and the Lord of lords.

Upon ascending into heaven, Christ was glorified with the glory that He had with the Father before the foundation of the world (John 17:5). However, there are important differences between His exalted state prior to the incarnation and His present exalted state in heaven. First of all, Christ now reigns as the God-Man. The One who sits upon the throne of the universe is flesh of His people's flesh and bone of their bone. Second, Christ now reigns as the Redeemer King. Through His death, He has redeemed a people for Himself from every tribe and tongue and people and nation, and they will reign with Him forever and ever (Revelation 5:9-10).

JESUS CHRIST IS KING

It is important to understand from the beginning that Christ is not merely *a* king or *like* a king; He is *the* King! In fact, He is the only true King that has ever been! All others who have reigned or will reign are merely faint shadows of His person and office.

1. There are many Old Testament prophecies that predicted that the coming Messiah would be a great King who would rule over the nations. Write your thoughts on the following prophecies.

   a. *Genesis 49:10*

   _____

   _____

   _____

   _____

   _____

NOTES: King David and the kings that succeeded him were descendants of the tribe of Judah. The Messiah was to come from this lineage (II Samuel 7:12-17). Jesus of Nazareth was a descendant of David (Matthew 1:1, 6; Romans 1:3). The Hebrew word *shiloh* is simply transliterated in the NASB. Most scholars translate it as "until he comes to whom it belongs" and interpret it as a reference to the Messiah, the great King of whom David was only a faint shadow or type.

b. *Numbers 24:17-18*

_____

_____

_____

_____

NOTES: In Balaam's final oracle, God gave him a revelation of the rise of the Messiah in the distant future. He would not only conquer and rule Moab and Edom, but would also possess and rule over all the nations.

c. *Micah 5:2*

_____

_____

_____

_____

NOTES: The prophet Micah predicted that a messianic "ruler" would be born in the same town as King David (I Samuel 16:1-13). However, the Messiah would be greater than David. Although He would be a Man from David's line, He would also be God, whose goings forth are from the days of eternity.

2. In II Samuel 7:16, a very special promise is given to David and his house (*i.e.* his descendants) regarding the establishment and endurance of his reign. In Luke 1:31-33, it is clear that this promise was fulfilled through Jesus Christ. Read both texts; explain how Jesus Christ is the fulfillment of the promise made to David.

_____

_____

_____

_____

_____

_____

_____

_____

NOTES: Jesus is not denying that the Father judges; He is explaining that He does so through His Son (Romans 2:16). The Father has given the Son power and authority to judge all of mankind. This great honor bestowed upon the Son is a demonstration of His deity and a reason for us to be careful to give the Son the honor that is due Him. According to verse 23, not only does the Father judge through the Son, but also mankind honors the Father through honoring the Son whom He has appointed as Judge. In Daniel 7:13-14, it was prophesied that the Son of Man (a designation for the Messiah) would be given dominion, glory, and a kingdom—all the peoples, nations, and men of every language would serve Him. His dominion would be an everlasting dominion that would never pass away or be destroyed. Jesus is that Son of Man.

3. We find still another powerful passage regarding Christ's divine appointment as Judge of all men in Acts 17:31. Read the text until you are familiar with its contents, and then write your thoughts.

_____

_____

_____

_____

_____

_____

NOTES: God has sovereignly established a day in which all mankind will be judged, and human history is rushing toward it. This judgment will not be arbitrary or unfair, but will be marked by perfect justice. God has not only appointed a Day of Judgment, but He has also appointed the Man through whom He will judge. That Man is His Son (see also Acts 10:42). The resurrection and ascension of Jesus of Nazareth is proof and validation that He is the Christ, the Son of God, the Supreme Lord, and the Judge of all creation.

THE RIGHTEOUS AND OMNISCIENT JUDGE

To be without error in His judgments, God must be perfectly righteous (without the slightest moral flaw) and omniscient (entirely aware of each and every fact).

The word "righteous" is translated from the Hebrew word **tsaddiq** and the corresponding Greek term **díkaios**. Both terms denote the rightness, correctness, or moral excellence of God. According to the Scriptures, God is an absolutely righteous Being and always acts in a way that is perfectly consistent with His nature. He will never be or do anything that would justify any accusation of wrongdoing. On the day when God judges all men through His Son Jesus Christ, even the condemned will bow their heads and declare that His judgment is right!

The word "omniscience" comes from the Latin word **omnisciens** [**omnis** = all + **sciens**, from **scire** = to know] and refers to the attribute of possessing all knowledge. God possesses a perfect knowledge of all things past, present, and future; and He possesses this knowledge immediately, effortlessly, simultaneously, and exhaustively. There is nothing hidden from Him. There is never the slightest difference between His knowledge and what actually is. He not only knows all the facts, but He also interprets each of them with perfect wisdom. On the Great Day of Judgment, Christ will judge every man according to His perfect knowledge of all the facts—no sin will be hidden or forgotten. Every creature, every deed, and every thought is always before Him like an open book.

1. In the Scriptures, a name has great significance in that it communicates something about the character of the one who bears it. What are the names given to the Lord Jesus Christ in the following Scriptures? What do these names communicate to us about the righteousness of Christ's judgment?

   a. *The H_____ and R_____ One (Acts 3:14).*

   _____

   _____

   _____

   _____

   _____

   b. *The R_____ J_____ (II Timothy 4:8).*

   _____

   _____

   _____

_____

_____

2. In Acts 17:31 is found an important promise regarding the character of God's judgment through His Son Jesus Christ. Identify this promise, and then explain its significance.

_____

_____

_____

_____

_____

_____

3. In order for the judgment of Christ to be perfectly just, He must be both righteous and omniscient. He must possess a perfect knowledge of the facts of every man's life. Does Christ possess sufficient knowledge to judge all men with perfect justice? What do the following Scriptures teach us regarding Christ's omniscience?

   a. *How does Christ describe Himself in Revelation 2:23? What does this description communicate to us about the thoroughness or exactness of His judgment?*

_____

_____

_____

_____

   b. *How does the Apostle Paul describe Christ's judgment in I Corinthians 4:4-5? What does this description communicate to us about the thoroughness or exactness of His judgment?*

_____

_____

_____

_____

_____

c. *What does the Apostle Paul declare in Romans 2:16 concerning the thoroughness and perfection of Christ's judgment? Will anything be hidden from Christ on the day He judges the world?*

_____

_____

_____

_____

_____

_____

Chapter 34: The Certainty of Judgment

We will bring our study of the gospel to a close with a consideration of the certainty of judgment and a brief description of it. In general, mankind seeks to avoid or even reject the biblical truth of a future judgment. Even among Christians, there is a tendency to ignore the subject in fear of being offensive. For this reason, we must constantly and consistently affirm that, according to the Scriptures and the teaching of Jesus Christ, there will be a future judgment that will determine the eternal destiny of every man. As we have already stated, to be true to Scripture, we must proclaim that the same Christ who came to die for the sins of His people will come a second time to judge and condemn those who have rejected His work of salvation.

THE CERTAINTY AND IMMINENCE OF JUDGMENT

The Scriptures declare that the coming judgment of the world through Jesus Christ is both certain and imminent. This judgment is **certain** because there is not even a shadow of a doubt in the Scriptures as to whether or not it will come to pass. There will be a judgment; and every man, from the first to the last, will be summoned and tried. This judgment is also **imminent** in that it could break upon the world at any moment. In the twinkling of an eye and when least expected, Christ will appear a second time; this time, however, it will not be to give His life as a sacrifice for sin, but to judge the world in righteousness and separate His people from those who refused to believe. It is for this reason that the Scriptures are filled with warnings concerning this Great Day and the need for all men to be prepared to meet their God!

1. The judgment of the world through the one Man whom God has appointed (Acts 17:31) is a great and unchangeable certainty. What does Romans 14:10-12 teach us about this truth?

_____

_____

_____

_____

_____

NOTES: In verse 11, God swears by His own person and name not only that everyone will be judged, but also that everyone will bow their knee and acknowledge both His authority to judge and the rightness of His judgment.

Made in the USA
Coppell, TX
22 June 2023